R.E. Mostell

A concise, incisive
pilgrimage through the
writings of a truly wholistic
physician

8/79

PERSONAL LIVING
An Introduction to Paul Tournier

MONROE PEASTON

PERSONAL LIVING

An Introduction to
Paul Tournier

HARPER & ROW, PUBLISHERS
New York, Evanston, San Francisco, London

For Phyllis

CONTENTS

Foreword

It is not often that one is asked to write a foreword for a book which is about oneself and one's work. It's unusual and embarrassing.

First, I am flattered that Professor Peaston has written a book about me, because he is a theologian while I am not, and because he studies what I write about psychology although I am not a psychiatrist. One shouldn't talk about flattery, however, because it allows one to talk in a more or less indifferent and impersonal tone, rather than admit how much one is flattered. Flattery makes one feel unable to be modest, but one must at least try to appear so.

I can do nothing about this first problem and there is another about which I feel even more perplexed. I have asked myself why the editors and author have asked me to write this foreword. Isn't it so that I will tell them whether I feel understood by the author, so that the readers may know if I feel correctly understood? But what does it mean to be understood and to feel understood?

The number of biographies of the same man determines the number of methods there will be to explain his life and his work. It is impossible for two men, no matter how alike, to understand me in the same way. It is also impossible for me to present myself in the same way to two different people. Each encounter is unique, because from the first words of our conversation, and even before we say anything, we influence each other by all that we already know and expect from each other. This interaction makes identical interpretation of a man impossible.

Each reader, reading these lines and then the book, will inevitably form for himself a different picture of me. And he will wonder if he has found in this foreword the same man about whom the author speaks later on. But the images can never exactly coincide. Georges Gusdorf has shown that the falsest biographies are autobiographies, even those written by the most careful and sincere authors.

What does this mean, if not that we all ask to be understood while we don't even understand ourselves. The thirst to be understood betrays in us a utopian aspiration to personal coherence, to a faithfulness to ourselves and a defined reality. We wish to be so consistent and yet we feel complex, changeable, indefinable, even contradictory. This is the problem of man's understanding of himself.

To try to understand others and help them to understand themselves is my profession—and my passion. Yet every day I see just how difficult that is, and how it remains unachieved. It seems even more difficult once one has discovered that we all carry within ourselves an enormous and inexhaustible subconscious, which endlessly contradicts our conscious selves but never completely takes complete power. I have also seen that one cannot progress in the comprehension of oneself all alone, but only by meeting with others in this game of mutual images which can never coincide.

In this difficult search for mutual understanding there are two paths: one synthetic and intuitive, and the other analytic and scientific. Once a man entered my office, and before I had even questioned him, before I even knew anything about him, he said, "I have faith in you, doctor, because you understand me." This means, "I have faith because you will understand me." And because he is confident, he speaks to me more openly than he has ever done before, which is precisely what allows

me to understand him better. He speaks the truth before it
even becomes true; he feels himself understood, a totally
intuitive feeling, primitive and direct.

This is precisely what I felt when Professor Peaston came to
see me in Geneva. I had at the onset the certitude of being
understood. And it is because of that that I willingly write this
foreword—not only because of all the work he has done to
understand me, but because of this link of mutual faith which
is the first condition of understanding.

This synthetic and fundamental understanding, however,
does not dismiss the value of a conscious and methodical effort
of analytic comprehension. The greater the naïve personal
communion, the more it throws us into the search for a more
detailed understanding, one which is more objective and
elaborate. It is important to remember, though, that in human
affairs, scientific understanding is never itself sufficient to give
the feeling of being understood, because it tends to make a
man the object of a study. It is an interpretation of a case
within the functions of a school of thought or doctrine, a
specific conception of man which allows a label to be placed
on the case but does not reach the person.

But when there is intuitive understanding, that of the heart,
then objective research becomes fruitful. That is why I thank
the author of such a serious work for being able to understand
me intellectually. I really feel that I am more of an intuitive
person than a thinker. A more knowledgeable man can usefully
complement me and explain in a more comprehensible way
the spirit of what I have so naïvely said.

What I wish to emphasize, finally, is the enormous need of
men to be understood and to feel that they are understood.
Why is it that the majority of them flatter themselves that
they understand others while so few feel understood by others?

If I have raised the point here of how understanding always
remains unachieved, I should add that in a sense this is good.
For what we wish, ultimately, is not so much to be understood

but to feel that another is continually searching to understand us—and that he will continue to try. When a husband, for example, after years of married life is convinced that he understands his wife, she will, more than ever, not feel understood; this is because her husband no longer seeks to understand in her anything which he has not already understood.

A book, then, is a search, an attempt to understand. Such a book is this one. And that reminds me of the beautiful prayer of St. Francis of Assisi: "I search to understand more than to be understood."

Geneva
December 31, 1971

PAUL TOURNIER

Preface

I first made the acquaintance of Paul Tournier when I read his book *The Meaning of Persons,* but it was not until 1961 that I met him in person when he and his wife visited North America. Later I found myself reading more of his books and directing students in the writing of theses on topics related to various aspects of his thought. Since I could not find any book which tried to present his thought and work as a whole, it occurred to me that I might write one myself.

I was encouraged to pursue this task by the thought that the many people who know Paul Tournier by one or more of his books might care to know something more about him and about his thought as a whole. Further, I sympathized with some of the questions he was raising because I was asking them myself. The interrelationship of psychiatry and religion, for example, has interested me for a long time largely because in my personal pilgrimage I owe much to both.

Much of the material that follows was prepared from reading Dr. Tournier's writings. In the biographical sections I am indebted to correspondence with him and to some personal interviews. I shall always remember with gratitude a short visit to Geneva when I was received with characteristic warmth and friendliness by Dr. and Mme. Tournier into their home at Troinex, a delightful rural community near the French border. They spoke to me of their family and friends and shared with me some of their ideas and aims. Since my French is a little less useable than Dr. Tournier's English, we both appreciated the presence of Professor Edmond Rochedieu of the University of Geneva. Later we continued our discussion in the presence of Pastor J. G. Bodmer, Director of the Ecumenical and Cultural Club of Geneva, and Mlle. Micheline Mitrani. All three interpreters added their own charm and helpfulness to our conversation.

I have tried here to expound the salient ideas which are to be found in Dr. Tournier's books and to relate these to his life and practice. Comment and criticism have been reserved for a final chapter. I have not attempted a criticism of details since it seemed far more important to make some general observations and reach an overall estimate.

At a later stage somebody may well prepare a much more exhaustive and definitive study. Such a work would rightly devote a good deal of space to a critical analysis of the ideas considered here. My purpose is rather different. I wish to introduce the man and his ideas. I hope to say enough about Paul Tournier and his thought as to encourage the reader to undertake his own exploration.

I wish to express my thanks to Professor G. Johnston, Dean of the Faculty of Religious Studies, McGill University, Montreal, and to the Faculty of Graduate Studies and Research, McGill University, for grants which relieved me of some of the cost of my visit to Geneva. In typing the manuscript my secretary, Miss H. M. Sinclair, has further increased my indebtedness to her.

I am grateful to the authors mentioned in the Notes, to Mr. H. Davis Yeuell and his colleagues at Harper & Row, and, of course, to Dr. Tournier himself for all that I have received. The responsibility for what is presented here, however, remains entirely mine.

Monroe Peaston

Montreal Diocesan Theological College
Montreal, Quebec

Abbreviations

References to Dr. Tournier's major writings and smaller works are simplified by means of the short titles indicated below. The French titles of the works and their dates of publication have been included. They appear in the order in which they were originally published although this order is not strictly followed in this presentation.

Healing
: *The Healing of Persons*
trans. Edwin Hudson (New York: Harper & Row, 1965). French title: *Médecine de la Personne,* 1940. Also translated into German, Danish, Spanish, Finnish, Dutch, Italian, Norwegian and Swedish.

Escape
: *Escape From Loneliness*
trans. John S. Gilmour (Philadelphia: Westminster Press, 1962). French title: *De la Solitude à la Communauté,* 1943. Also translated into German, Danish, Finnish, Italian, Norwegian, Swedish, Dutch and Japanese.

Reborn
: *The Person Reborn*
trans. Edwin Hudson (New York: Harper & Row, 1966). French title: *Technique et Foi,* 1944. Also translated into German, Dutch, Norwegian, Swedish and Spanish.

Broken World
: *The Whole Person in a Broken World*
trans. John and Helen Doberstein (New York: Harper & Row, 1964). French title: *Désharmonie de la Vie Moderne,* 1947. Also translated into German, Italian, Norwegian and Swedish.

Strong   *The Strong and the Weak*
and Weak   trans. Edwin Hudson (Philadelphia: Westminster
                Press, 1963). French title: *Les Forts et les Faibles,*
                1948. Also translated into German, Dutch, Swedish,
                Finnish and Japanese.

Casebook   *A Doctor's Casebook in the Light of the Bible*
                trans. Edwin Hudson (New York: Harper & Row,
                1960). French title: *Bible et Médecine,* 1951. Also
                translated into German, Spanish, Finnish, Dutch,
                Italian, Norwegian, Swedish and Japanese.

Meaning   *The Meaning of Persons*
                trans. Edwin Hudson (New York: Harper & Row,
                1957). French title: *Le Personnage et la Personne,*
                1955. Also translated into German, Finnish, Greek,
                Dutch, Italian, Norwegian, Swedish and Chinese.

Guilt   *Guilt and Grace*
and Grace   trans. A. W. Heathcote assisted by J. J. Henry and
                P. J. Allcock (New York: Harper & Row, 1962).
                French title: *Vraie ou Fausse Culpabilité,* 1958. Also
                translated into German, Finnish and Dutch.

Seasons   *The Seasons of Life*
                trans. John S. Gilmour (Richmond, Virginia: John
                Knox Press, 1963). French title: *Cadeaux, Pour-
                Vie,* 1961. Also translated into German, Finnish
                and Japanese.

Gifts   *The Meaning of Gifts*
                trans. John S. Gilmour (Richmond, Virginia: John
                Knox Press, 1963). French title: *Des Cadeaux, pour-
                quoi?,* 1961. Also translated into German and Fin-
                nish.

Resist or   *To Resist or To Surrender*
Surrender   trans. John S. Gilmour (Richmond, Virginia: John
                Knox Press, Chime Paperback, 1969). French title:
                Tenir tête ou céder, 1962. Also translated into Ger-
                man and Finnish.

To Understand   *To Understand Each Other*
                trans. John S. Gilmour (Richmond, Virginia: John
                Knox Press, 1967). French title: *Difficultés Conju-*

gales, 1962. Also translated into German, Dutch, Japanese, Finnish, Spanish and Iranian.

Secrets   *Secrets*
trans. Joe Embry (Richmond, Virginia: John Knox Press, 1965). French title: *Le Secret,* 1963. Also translated into German and Finnish.

Adventure   *The Adventure of Living*
trans. Edwin Hudson (New York: Harper & Row, 1965). French title: *L'Aventure de la Vie,* 1963. Also translated into Finnish and German.

Place   *A Place for You*
trans. Edwin Hudson (New York: Harper & Row, 1968). French title: *L'Homme et son lieu,* 1966. Also translated into German and Italian.

1 ❖ A Doctor's Formation

If you meet Paul Tournier, read his books, or examine his life and work, a clear impression will be left on your mind. He is a friendly man, humane and compassionate, who has an intense conviction of the grandeur, aliveness, and grace of God. His faith has undergirded and inspired his life and work and has expanded his understanding of the world and of man. The natural world and the laws of its operation are as much within the providence of God as is the grace of Jesus Christ of which revealed religion speaks. So, too, are the psychophysical and personal aspects of man's nature open to God. Man is a unitary being and must be understood in his totality and uniqueness.

This approach to human nature has made Paul Tournier critical of modern medicine insofar as it tries to be purely objective and scientific. Educated in this school and obliged to follow its methods and procedures in his work as a general practitioner, Tournier realized that there are many factors in the lives of his patients that contribute either to the origin or the course of their illness but that lie beyond the reach of medical science. Valid and valuable as this tool is, it seemed to meet only part of his patients' needs. Tournier found himself obliged to take into account his patients' inner anxieties, psychological and personal needs, and creative possibilities as well as their physical complaints. The patients' basic orientation to life—their deepest convictions about its worth and direction—

seemed as important and as necessary to correct as their physical malfunction and psychological conflicts.

Confronted by this situation and taught largely by his own
personal and religious experience, Tournier realized that the
most satisfactory way he could exercise the art of healing was
to combine medical knowledge, psychological understanding,
and religious insight. To this task he has devoted himself for
more than thirty years.

2

Paul Tournier is the son of Louis Tournier (1828–1898). A
staunch Calvinist and a strong opponent of liberal tendencies
in theology, Louis Tournier was appointed pastor to the
Cathedral of St. Peter in Geneva. At that time the cathedral
was the center of a single, large parish. As pastor and preacher,
Tournier was widely known and respected. During this period
he also published several poems.[1]

In his forties, however, Tournier began to exhibit symptoms
of an emotional disorder. His distress increased after the death
in 1883 of his first wife, to whom he had been married happily
for twenty years. The ill-health which beset him obliged him
to give up the ministry of preaching and to assume the duties
of a religious instructor. His addresses to children proved to
be exceedingly popular and attracted many older people
as well.

In 1890 Louis Tournier married Elizabeth Ormond, a woman
of twenty-eight who had been his student. A daughter, Louise,
was born in 1894, and a son, Paul, was born in 1898.

Three months after Paul's birth, Louis Tournier died in the
village of Troinex, near Geneva. Elizabeth died six years later,
in 1904, after a lingering illness. Her brother, Jacques Ormond,
a banker, and his wife, took the two orphans into their home.
Mme. Ormond, a devout and generous woman, was not without her limitations as a foster mother, though she exercised a

considerable influence on the religious life of her two wards. She too showed signs of mental illness and physical disability, infirmities that the two children found even more confusing than the loss of their parents. This was particularly true of Paul who continued to retreat into a fantasy world of his own, hiding away in his tree hut or talking to his uncle's dogs.

In Tournier's books there are several references to his early experience as an orphan. It has left an indelible impression upon him despite the self-awareness he shows in relation to it. He and his mother were deeply attached to each other, she having lost a husband much older than herself, he having been denied the presence and support of a father. The death of his mother when he was six bred in Paul Tournier a sense of the harshness of life. He began to feel that he did not count in anyone's eyes and that no one was interested in him. Solitude became his refuge and shyness his characteristic trait. Yet within his mind, even at this early age, a resolve was taking shape: He would defeat that monster, death, that had taken his mother from him. By the age of twelve that resolve had become a conscious commitment. He was going to be a doctor.

Meanwhile, his uncle, Jacques, did his utmost to keep before the boy's mind the image of his father. Paul's response could only be ambivalent: He would be like his father, yet different from him; he would exercise a cure of souls, but not in the same way his father had.

The importance of Jacques Ormond in Paul's life may be gauged by the profound impact of his uncle's death in an automobile accident in the south of France in 1935. Dr. and Mme. Tournier and their two sons were in the car at the time; Tournier was the driver. He and his sons escaped injury; Mme. Tournier was badly hurt, but Jacques Ormond was killed. The poignancy of guilt and the meaning of forgiveness was brought home to him in a remarkable way. The experience was to receive careful examination later in his writings about guilt and grace.

3

Although Tournier proved to be an indifferent pupil, save in mathematics, at the private school and high school (college) which he attended in Geneva, he developed exceedingly well as a medical student at the University. As a teen-ager he formed one significant relationship to which several references are made in his books. His Greek teacher, Jules Dubois, realized how much his shy pupil needed friendship. Accordingly, Dubois invited him to his home, held discussions with him, and made him feel that his ideas were worth listening to. Although these conversations were largely intellectual, they helped Tournier realize his ability in handling ideas. This encouraged him to mix socially with others, for he could at least hold his own at an intellectual level. He quickly became a leader among his companions at the University of Geneva and was elected president of the Society of Zofingue, a country-wide student body.

While Tournier's escape from shyness and loneliness was only partial at this time, at least he was moving in the right direction. A further step was taken after World War I when he assisted the International Red Cross in repatriating Russian and Austrian prisoners of war. This work took him to Vienna and to other parts of Eastern Europe.

After graduating in medicine at the University of Geneva, Tournier went to Paris for a year's internship (1923). He returned to Geneva for a longer internship of four years at the Polyclinic. At the end of this period (1928) he entered private practice in Geneva and continued in it until his recent retirement. Throughout his professional career Tournier remained a general practitioner. He has never had specialist training in psychiatry and disclaims the title of psychiatrist, although he has read widely and thought deeply in the field of psychology and psychological medicine.

4

Tournier considers that prior to 1932 he was an idealist and a devoted supporter of the Christian ethic. The son of Louis Tournier, he could hardly have escaped the influence of Calvin's thought and work. His careful study of Calvin's writings impressed him with the solidarity and coherence of this profound theological system.

Intellectual assent to theological propositions did not, however, bring to Tournier a living faith. That came when he encountered members of a new religious movement, the Oxford Group, who paid a visit to Geneva in 1932. The effect of this encounter on him was so momentous that we shall devote the next chapter to it. At this point it is sufficient to say that the religious experience into which he entered as a result of this meeting gave a new direction to his life and work. It led him to develop and to practice what he himself has called the medicine of the person, a cure of souls (*une guérison de l'âme*), in which medical knowledge, psychological understanding, and religion are combined.

In August 1937, Tournier felt that he ought to inform his patients of the new direction his work would take. In a letter to them, he pointed out that he had embarked on a career in medicine in order to be of help to his fellows.[2] His work would take him beyond the diagnosis and treatment of physical complaints to the deeper problems within the personalities of his patients and to the study of human personality in its entirety.

Man, he noted in his letter, is a unitary being. In origin he is a single cell which subdivides over and over again. Yet the underlying unity remains. When an organ of the body is diseased, it is a sign that something is out of harmony with the whole. Differential diagnosis is important, yet it has to be remembered that it is within the whole individual that the drama of illness occurs.

Tournier set himself the task of inquiring into the nature of personality as a whole. Within the scope of his investigations were such topics as heredity, temperament, natural vitality, way of living, diet, activities, leisure, inner conflicts, values, and the person's fundamental response to his place in the world. This preliminary outline of the medicine of the person was extended and developed in Tournier's first book, *The Healing of Persons,* which was widely read and well received in Europe. Some physicians, who read it during World War II, either wrote to him asking for additional direction or visited him for further discussion. Tournier and others were beginning to see the need for a more personal, less specialized, and more humane medicine.

In May 1946, Tournier and his wife took part in the first Evangelical Academy at Bad Boll in Germany. The idea of holding this meeting originated with a young German theologian who felt that doctors and theologians should meet to work out in dialogue a new approach to healing founded on the gospel. The meeting of the Evangelical Academy gave Tournier the clue he was seeking. In the summer of 1947, A. Maeder, a psychiatrist from Zurich, J. de Rougement, a surgeon from Lyon (both members of the Oxford Group at the time), and Tournier organized a meeting of doctors to consider their common purposes. So that the organization might not come under the jurisdiction of any particular church but yet have a Christian connection, they asked Dr. W. A. Visser 't Hooft, then General Secretary of the World Council of Churches, if the Chateau de Bossey (near Geneva) might be put at their disposal. He readily agreed.

Thus the Bossey Group came into being. On the advice of the theologian Emil Brunner, ecclesiastics and theologians were not invited lest their presence should make the discussions too abstract. It was felt, too, that doctors who had some doubts about Christian dogma might talk more readily among themselves if theologians were not present. The doctors invited to

the meeting were united by one concern: to resist the excessive
specialization of medicine insofar as it tended to depersonalize
the patient. They wanted to cultivate the medicine of the
person.

At first Tournier felt that biblical instruction and the use
of the liturgy should be avoided. It was soon realized, however,
that the purposes of the group might become obscured under
a cloud of vague idealism. The humane medicine they were
seeking raised questions of a spiritual order and called for
more specific direction. After 1948, Tournier, with the en-
couragement of his colleagues, prepared studies for the Bossey
Group on the biblical basis of medicine. Two of his books,
A Doctor's Casebook in the Light of the Bible and *Guilt and
Grace,* are drawn from studies originally presented to the
Bossey Group.

The Group still exists and meets annually. Tournier attends
and naturally enjoys the authority of an elder statesman,
though a dedicated team of young doctors has now become responsible for its direction.

2 ❖ Decisive Encounter

Although Tournier's early life was deeply influenced by his father's work as a pastor, preacher, and catechist in Geneva, he seems to have been a stranger to the Christian faith as experienced in true commitment and feeling. The young Tournier held that the Church was a valuable institution as a repository and teacher of Christian truth, and he himself was prepared to defend it as an intellectual creed. It was for him a topic to be discussed rather than a way of life. This was true of Tournier during his later student days and early professional career despite his humanitarian zeal in the service of the International Red Cross among war prisoners. He had not yet coordinated and harmonized credal affirmation, humanitarian service, and vital personal experience.

Tournier's loyalty to the Church as an institution, however, did not allow him to remain uncritical. Such an attitude is not unusual among sons of the manse and is by no means absent from present-day postulants to the ministry. In response to the appeal of a friend, he joined a group of lay people and ministers who wished to discover ways to revive a Church that seemed in many respects to be backward and unattractive to youth. The group became known as the "Restless Youth of the Church." Plans for reform were devised, and Tournier was able to act as spokesman for this group when, in due course, he became a member of the Consistory of the Church.

One result of the group's activity was the visit of a team

of evangelists to Geneva. Their message and influence left Tournier with a feeling of uneasiness. The disparity between his profession of faith and his inner experience was brought home to him with even greater force. He began to feel that he was in greater need of religious renewal rather than the Church.

It was at this point, in 1932, that Tournier first met members of a new religious movement known as the Oxford Group. Tournier was thirty-four at the time. His attention had been drawn to the movement by a striking transformation that had occurred in the life of a former patient. Tournier was told that this woman, who had been aggressive and self-opinionated, had become considerate, humble, and devoted to the good of others, and this change was attributed to the influence of the Oxford Group. Resolved to discover how this had come about, Tournier was introduced to some of its prominent members, including a theologian, Emil Brunner, a psychiatrist from Zurich, Dr. Alphonse Maeder, and a literary man, Professor Spoerri.

Tournier hoped to receive from them an exposition of the principles and methods of the new movement. Instead, he found himself listening to a series of anecdotes which illustrated the ways in which these men had been challenged to change their attitudes and way of life. Tournier later admitted that he found this procedure exasperating. His taste for intellectual discussion went unrespected, for it is hard to argue with a series of challenging incidents. He was sufficiently irritated with the meeting to inform those present that he had come asking for bread and had been given a stone!

Such was Tournier's first encounter with a religious movement that was to exercise a radical and far-reaching influence on his life. In view of this fact, it will be helpful to spend a moment or two glancing at this movement and particularly at its founder, F. N. D. Buchman, since the Oxford Group can best be appreciated against the background of his history, personality, and achievement.[1]

2

Frank Nathan Daniel Buchman (1878–1961) was nurtured in a conservative Lutheran family in Pennsylvania. He was graduated from a Lutheran seminary before undertaking work as a minister at Overbrook, Pennsylvania, near Philadelphia.

At the age of thirty, Buchman visited Keswick, England (1908), where he underwent a remarkable religious experience. A woman's address to a small congregation proved to be a turning point in his life. "I had entered the little church," he later reported, "with a divided will, nursing pride, selfishness, ill-will, which prevented me from functioning as a Christian minister should. The woman's simple talk personalized the Cross for me that day, and suddenly I had a poignant vision of the Crucified."[2] Frank Buchman found his dividedness overcome as he made an act of total surrender to Christ. And he was deeply stirred by a strong wave of emotion. "I left that service," he remarked, "with a consciousness of having the complete answer to all my difficulties and sins. . . ."[3]

He returned to America to embark on a fruitful career as an evangelist among college students, first under the auspices of the Y.M.C.A. at Pennsylvania State University, and as extension lecturer in Personal Evangelism at Hartford Seminary (1916–1922). Later, he gave up this salaried post to inaugurate a religious movement for "world changing through life changing."

Earlier, as part of his Lutheran heritage, Buchman had entered into the pietist tradition which emerged so vigorously in the late seventeenth century, largely as a result of the work of Philip Jacob Spener (1635–1705) and his followers. In his *Pia Desideria*[4] (*Pious Aspirations*), Spener had strongly criticized the shortcomings of the Church, its moral laxity and preoccupation with arid religious controversy, and had urged the cultivation of Christian virtue by means of small groups meeting for biblical study and edification. K. S. Latourette has summarized the matter: "Spener was intent upon a moral and spiritual reformation. He was grieved by controversy over doctrine. . . . he stressed . . . genuine conversion and the cultivation of the Christian life. . . . He discounted doctrinal sermons, [and] preached the necessity of the new birth, a personal, warm, Christian experience, and the cultivation of Christian virtues."[5]

These were precisely Buchman's objectives as he began his work among American college students. The particular methods he adopted for achieving them were partly of his own devising and partly due to the influence of Henry Wright of Yale (1877–1923), who proclaimed the need for life change, the observance of the "morning watch," and the affirmation of the moral absolutes—honesty, purity, unselfishness, and love. Buchman brought these ideas with him into his new movement, but he gave them a shape of his own as he viewed them in the light of his Keswick experience.

On returning to his Keswick boarding house after the church service, Buchman wrote several letters of apology to the trustees of a settlement house in Philadelphia with whom he was at loggerheads. He also "shared" with a member of the household where he was staying the remarkable experience he had just undergone. Thereafter, restitution and sharing were to become prevailing emphases in his new movement.

To these influences we must add Buchman's personal qualities: tireless energy, considerable powers as an organiser, and a desire for achievement—all combined to make Frank Buchman a man of notable managerial ability. His aptness as a spiritual diagnostician and his powers of discernment in character not only gave him immense influence over young men caught in the conflicts of adolescence, but enabled him to enlist the services of gifted individuals as his lieutenants. In this latter capacity he may also have been aided by a naïve fascination for important, or supposedly important, people.

Indifferent to ecclesiastical structures and theologically simplistic, Buchman opened himself to the criticisms of men like Hensley Henson (Bishop of Durham, 1920–1939) who charged him with ignoring the demands of the intellect. "If the Religion of the Incarnation is to justify its theory, it must satisfy the requirements of the educated intellect as well as bring peace to the troubled conscience, satisfaction to the aspirations of the spirit, and guidance in the various perplexities of secular life."[6] But, at the same time, Buchman's emphasis on feeling and will in religious experience brought a much needed corrective for those who found in it only reason and understanding.

Buchman's intense religious life was his dominant characteristic. To him, God was a living, personal reality who has a plan for every human life, a plan that he will communicate to those who seek him sincerely and obediently. Such communication could be as clear and unmistakable as when a man speaks with his friends. That is why the quiet time, the hour of meditation, with its opportunity for unhurried, silent reflection before God, was so important to Buchman and to those who were influenced by him.

3

A. J. Russell has a clear outline of the religious experience so often found in Buchman's movement: "First, there was absolute Surrender, including Faith in the Cross of Christ, bringing Guidance by the Holy Spirit; then there was Sharing, bringing true Fellowship and shining faces; then Life-Changing, bringing in God's Kingdom and Joy, in Heaven, in the Sinner, and in the Life-Changer; then Faith and Prayer. . . ; also those four standards of Love, Honesty, Purity and Unselfishness, on which Christ had never compromised; and, of course, Restitution. Later I was to understand perhaps the strongest principle of all—Fearless Dealing with Sin. Mean-

while, there were two other principles easier to swallow—
Team-work and Loyalty."[7]

Thus, the chief features of this religious experience were
the changed life, guidance sought and given in the quiet hour
of meditation, adherence to the four absolutes, and sharing
and loyalty within the group fellowship. It was assumed that
everyone had some fault or sin of which he was secretly
ashamed. Challenged at this point, one could be brought to
acknowledge the reality of this sin and its harmful effects. "Sin
blinds, sin binds, sin multiplies, sin dulls and deadens our
highest sensitivities." Such statements were frequently repeated.
"The best definition of sin that we have is that sin is anything in my life which keeps me from God and other people."[8]
To acknowledge this situation, to admit one's failure to meet
the moral ideal, to offer apology or to make restitution to those
with whom one has been at odds, and then to surrender one's
life unreservedly to God's direction, was to experience a change
in life in its most far-reaching sense.

The surrendered and changed life had then to become open
to Divine direction. This called for unhurried quiet before
God in moments of meditation when God's guidance could be
sought and received. Such guidance could always be checked
by reference to others in the Group or to the absolutes of
honesty, purity, unselfishness, and love. It should not be
thought that guidance was only of a general kind; it could be
direct, detailed, and definite, a pointer towards a way of acting
in present circumstances. To apply the four absolutes after
guidance had been given was a most searching test.

Sharing within the group fellowship could be a means of
checking guidance; it could also be an act of confession as
something profitable in itself or as a means of witness. In this
sense it was a "confession of faults long since overcome by a
'changed' individual for the purpose of encouraging prospec-
tive converts."[9] Sharing of this sort naturally engendered a
deep sense of loyalty to the group fellowship. The maintenance

of that loyalty became an overriding demand for those who
continued in it, particularly for those who engaged in international missions as part of a visiting team.

The dangers of this kind of experience, however, are not difficult to recognize. Buchman's preoccupation with the wealthy
and the great, the Group's tendency to exercise a religious
dictatorship, its theological inadequacy and naïveté on the subject of guidance—these are some of the criticisms which have
been leveled against it. It cannot be denied, however, that this
movement brought to many a disciplined, personal religion
which was quite new in their experience. It demonstrated
widely the meaning of Christianity and offered to thousands
an enduring spiritual fellowship. Silent meditation brought a
fresh orientation to life, and sharing yielded a sense of be-
longing to a worthwhile group. "It has been a flowering of the
great Protestant tradition with its emphasis on the individual
and its willingness to let the individual speak out of his own
authority. . . ."[10]

4

Having considered the message and aims of the Oxford
Group, we return to Tournier's first encounter with it. There
was an important sequel to that first meeting. Among those
present on that occasion was Jan van Walré de Bordes, a Dutch
financier and a highly placed official in the League of Nations
at Geneva. A recent convert to the Group, de Bordes had
spoken of his experience of morning meditation when, in
silence, he opened himself to God and listened attentively so
as to receive divine guidance.

Tournier was so impressed with this testimony that he attempted the same procedure the next morning. His first attempt was not very rewarding, but he felt impelled to continue
the practice. Thus he began the habit of having a period of
daily reflection, a practice which has had a profound influence
on his life and career.

Equally significant was Tournier's subsequent private conversation with de Bordes. For the first time Tournier found himself in the presence of a man who candidly shared with him his experiences of life whether they were flattering or not. Bordes's ability to do this encouraged Tournier. Immediately he experienced a remarkable feeling of liberation; he was freed from the intellectual stronghold in which he had taken refuge for so long. The cathartic effect of emotional release was profound. In his youth his Greek teacher had initiated him into the first level of personal meeting, that of intellectual discussion. The present emotional release had even more far-reaching effects. It began to revolutionize his relationship with his wife, his children, and his patients, and as we have indicated, it affected the course of his career.

Speaking in Oslo in 1969 Tournier remarked: "The thing that led me to psychotherapy was the experience I had when I began to talk to some of my patients in a personal way."[11] He discovered that when he shared with a patient something of himself, some life situation that had been significant to him, the patient became aware of some life problem which was related to his illness either in its origin or in its progress. The patient was encouraged by his physician's example to speak freely of matters which had unconsciously bothered him for a long time. Such deep and spontaneous disclosures usually had a remarkable healing effect.

Tournier and his patients experienced a transference of feeling to which psychoanalysis has attached great importance. Only later, as a result of studying psychoanalysis and psychology, did Tournier appreciate the theory underlying this fact. Like many before him, Tournier experienced the actuality of transference before he became aware of the theory.

Another interesting experience befell Tournier as a result of practicing silent meditation. He found that he could relax in the loving, all-embracing presence of God in such a way that the psychological "censor" withdrew, thus permitting an awareness of hidden memories and repressed desires. He began to reach a new level of self-awareness as he continued on his way toward the discovery of inner truth without which no man can be free. The guidance he received in his hour of meditation related not only to what he should do but also to how he should be.

5

In the late 1930s, after a series of annual house parties had been held at Oxford and elsewhere and a number of ministry teams had visited South Africa, Canada, the United States, and countries in Europe and the Far East, the Oxford Group decided to change its name. It became known as Moral Rearmament (MRA). There was now a greater emphasis on labor-management relationships and on international affairs. "Moral Rearmament is not an organization," remarked Peter Howard, "a sect, or a religion. It is an ideology. It is the way men live and what they live for."[12]

This new trend toward political and social action did not suit Tournier who, for some time before World War II and certainly after it, was preoccupied with different concerns. His interest was in the healing of persons, in the relationship between faith and science, and in finding in medicine a broader approach toward its task of prevention and treatment. Above all, he recognized the basic importance of man's response to the living God. This emphasis had been central in the best days of the Oxford Group, but the spirit of the movement appeared to have changed. There was a new authoritarianism abroad, a demand for disciplined obedience to the team. This made some of the more sensitive people feel they were being "used." Tournier decided to sever his ties with MRA. It was a hard decision to reach. The pressure to retain his loyalty seemed strong while he himself felt weak. His book *The Strong and the Weak* reflects in part his struggle at the time.

It is only fair, however, to recall the permanent benefit which came to Tournier as a result of an association with this movement over a period of fourteen years (1932–1946). It was the means of introducing him to a personal, vital religious experience. He began to enjoy a new openness to God as a forgiving, healing, and guiding presence in the midst of life. It brought him emotional release and consequent personal growth through the practice of sharing. It led him to undertake written meditation through which he has found not only guidance for living but an altogether deeper self-awareness. It encouraged his reflection upon the Bible whose message has informed his life, his practice, and his writing.

Sharing and meditation introduced him to psychotherapy and to a new emphasis in his career. His medical practice became a "cure of souls" in which psychology and religion have been combined. Even the anecdotal approach of the first members of the Group whom he met has influenced his written style. Ideas and anecdotes are combined in his books in a remarkable way.

Above all, it enlarged his understanding of human nature and his conception of the task of healing. He preserved and applied rigorously everything he had learned from scientific medicine, but, in addition, he became sufficiently open to personal dialogue with his patients as to encourage the disclosure to him of their deepest thoughts and feelings.

And finally, association with the Oxford Group had convinced Tournier of the value of fellowship and teamwork in furthering any enterprise. He applied this lesson immediately in the cause of the medicine of the person by founding the Bossey Group.

3 ❖ The Medicine of the Person

In the period immediately prior to World War II, Tournier found himself obliged to reconsider the meaning of his vocation and the direction of his life in the light of the profound influence of Buchman's teaching. The letter sent to his patients in 1937 outlined the stance he would adopt, but true to the Group tradition into which he had entered, he needed to work out its details on paper. Service in the military during World War II delayed publication of his manuscript until 1940. The book is entitled *Médecine de la Personne*. The English edition appeared under the title *The Healing of Persons* and contained the dedicatory note: "To Dr. Frank N. D. Buchman, whose teaching has had a profound influence on my personal life and has obliged me to reflect upon the true meaning of my vocation."

The book does not claim to present a systematic exposition of Tournier's theory of healing. Systematic presentation was not, and is not, his style.[1] It is a collection of anecdotes, experiences, and ideas that he had shaped into a coherent whole as he wrestled with the question of his vocation. The work is not merely an exercise in self-clarification; it has its own serious intention. "For the real meaning of this book, the meaning I intend it to have, is that it should be a contribution, in the medical sphere, to the spiritual renewal which our world needs" (*Healing* p. 287).

The work is Tournier's attempt to see the practice of medicine in the light of his own religious renewal; it was an exposition of that "spiritually oriented medicine" (*Healing* p. 10) which he now felt called to follow. He has attached great importance to the book, not only because it was widely received in Europe, but mainly because it expressed those convictions which have colored his subsequent thinking. This was his "cry of the heart," and its tones echo through his later work and writing. As a sort of "apology for his life," its main emphases need to be appreciated if Tournier is to be understood.

2

It was natural that a reflecting physician begin with the notion of health and healing. Health he conceived to be "a quality of life, a physical, psychical, and spiritual unfolding, < an exaltation of personal dynamism" (*Healing* p. 185). There is an urge to wholeness or completeness within the person which reaches its fulfillment as a person becomes fully func- – tioning in every aspect of his nature. Given such a state of affairs, the condition of health exists.

This point of view is similar to that adopted by one of Tournier's contemporaries, Leslie D. Weatherhead, who also was concerned with the meaning of health and healing. "*Health*," wrote Weatherhead, "*is the complete and successful functioning of every part of the human being, in harmonious relationship with every other part and with the relevant environment.*"[2]

But what is involved in bringing about this state of affairs? This was Tournier's basic question. *The Healing of Persons* and his lifework have been an attempt to answer it. Of two things he was completely convinced. First, he was sure that an atomistic medical approach, though pressed with the utmost scientific rigor, could never of itself be an adequate healing instrument. "Man . . . is a unity: body, mind, and spirit. . . . To treat a man is to treat him, therefore, in his entirety" (*Healing* p. 136). Second, he held that it was false to assume that there was only one direction of causal relationship within the human organism. "It is an unscientific assumption of materialist philosophy which supposes that the material facts—anatomical and physiological—are the cause, and that the moral (psychological and spiritual) facts are the consequence, and not the other way round. . . . This causal relationship seems to me to be always reciprocal, that is to say that the material facts are as much the cause as the consequence of the spiritual facts, and vice versa" (*Healing* pp. 132–133). Thus health is bound up not only with the condition of a man's physical organism but also with his way of life, with his mode of being in the world, and with his fundamental orientation to life.

Treatment, then, calls for a twofold approach, since man's nature is both psychophysical and personal. He is a body, which possesses its own closely knit and interrelated systems (skeletal, circulatory, nervous, and so forth); he is a mind (or psyche), with his own needs, emotions, perceptions, memory, and intelligence; and he is a personal center of freedom and responsibility. The body, including the brain, can indeed be the object of scientific investigation, as can the mind with its own dynamic structures and mechanisms. But as a personal center man is more elusive, although the key to any understanding of him as a unitary being lies here. Only personal dialogue can disclose the central needs of the person.

Such a twofold approach meant, for example, that one patient's digestive troubles called for traditional forms of history-taking, examination, diagnosis, and treatment, but they also had to be considered in relation to his divided loyalty. He was a married man and yet was having an affair with another woman (*Healing* p. 6). Another patient's menstrual difficulties needed to be relieved by a course of ovarian extract, but the fact that she had been the victim of attempted rape brought emotional overtones to her condition (*Healing* p. 7).

In yet another case, Tournier noticed that during the patient's second sojourn in the mountains for high-altitude treatment, his condition not only improved rapidly but his attitude changed considerably. His rebellion had given way to acceptance (*Healing* p. 18–20). Such an observation bears a close resemblance to one of the conclusions drawn in an English study of tuberculous patients. "The data strongly suggest that the speed and chance of recovery of an individual depend to a great extent on his personality, and that sometimes it may be safer to assess a patient's prognosis on the basis of his personality and of his emotional conflicts than on the basis of the shadow on the film."[3]

As part of this approach, however, it must be remembered that a person has become what he is in virtue of the terrain he possesses and the history he has had. By terrain, Tournier means the constitution of the person insofar as it is determined by hereditary factors. Just as a tract of country will exhibit distinctive features and configuration, so "personality must be considered to possess an inherited nucleus, a nucleus of physical and psychological potentialities."[4] This biological substratum, the temperament of a person, his native drive, and his prevailing mood will be closely associated. By history Tournier means those nurtural and environmental influences of the person's past which culture, society, and the family have combined to exert.

At this stage in his career Tournier had a particular interest in the terrain, or physiological and temperamental basis, of personality. He has not been alone in this interest. Kretschmer, for example, had noted connections between the physique of the frail, linear, narrowly built person (asthenic type), the firmly built, vigorous, muscular person (athletic type), the short, plump, rounded individual (pyknic type), the people who exhibit digressions from the average (dysplastic types), and their general mood, behavioral response, and tendency to mental disorder.[5]

In Tournier's list the choleric individual represents the alert, active, energetic go-getter who rises naturally to the challenge of decision and leadership. The melancholic person, on the other hand, is more thoughtful in his approach and more emotionally sensitive in his response. The sanguine person is imaginative, expansive, optimistic, bent on one quest after another, while the lymphatic (or phlegmatic) type is gentle, conscientious, and passive (*Healing* pp. 66–81).

It has been fashionable to question this kind of typology, partly because it favors rigid and static concepts, rather than those which are fluid and dynamic, and partly because it does not do justice to the uniqueness of the individual. Although the truth of these objections must be allowed, there is ground for affirming that "typologies are not altogether arbitrary, do not necessarily do violence to the manifoldness of the human, but have some basis in the structure of psychological reality."[6]

This kind of approach was important to Tournier because it enabled him to distinguish carefully between temperament and character, among body structure, accompanying emotional tone, general response (what is given), and the *quality* of the person (that for which he bears some responsibility). He held this kind of distinction to be essential for self-acceptance. A man can know and accept his make-up for what it is; at the same time he can recognize that the mood and behavioral response of others may be part of their temperament and may therefore not be a matter for reproach or blame. Tournier himself admits to having reproached his wife for her pessimism and apprehensiveness as proof of her lack of faith. He later found it wise not to confuse pessimism with unbelief nor to mistake optimism for faith. "For my own part, I prided myself on my optimistic outlook as if it came from my faith and not from my inborn disposition" (*Healing* p. 79).

It is as important, however, to know how a person *responds* to his given terrain, and to his nurture, as to know what his terrain and nurture are. He may take flight from the realities of his make-up and of his life, or he may accept them. If he is an escapist he may take flight into accidents (accident-proneness), repetitive illnesses, or the use of medication, alcohol, or drugs. Addictions of various kinds, Tournier notes, "are the visible symptoms of personal moral problems such as feelings of inferiority, shyness, idleness, sexual difficulties, and weak will" (*Healing* p. 107). Here, however, the flight is not so much from the realities of what is given as from the harmful effects of one's nurture. No nurtural process occurs without bringing about a condition of inner conflict within the individual, the components of which are often beyond conscious awareness. In respect of such conflicts evasive and escapist tactics may be employed.

Indeed, religion itself may be a form of escape. "The religious life itself can be an escape; an escape into a little mystic chapel . . . where one can hide in order to escape the world and its wounds, to wallow in a passive enjoyment that is pointless and out of contact with reality" (*Healing* p. 108).

Acceptance of one's life is the more favorable response. This involves a positive and welcoming attitude toward one's sex and sexuality, toward marriage and one's marriage partner, toward children, toward the single state, and toward the decline in vigor and range of interests that comes with increasing age. But it covers far more. "Accepting one's life means accepting all that one considers to be unfair victimization, the injustices of fate as well as those of men" (*Healing* p. 165).

Even toward a deviation like homosexuality, this attitude is best. "Acceptance of one's nature as it is, with its infirmities and the difficulties they entail, acceptance of them without rebellion, is one of the demands Christianity makes. . . . This particular infirmity [homosexuality] is to be regarded in the same way as all the others, which are compatible with happiness insofar as they are not rebelled against" (*Healing* p. 182).

4

Tournier saw the choice between flight and acceptance as bound inseparably with an attitude of openness and trust toward the realm of the spirit. A man, as a personal center of freedom and responsibility, may enter into a close relationship with God. Victories won in this dimension bear fruit in the physical and psychological state of the person, not least in his capacity to accept himself for what he is (cf. *Healing* p. 61).

One patient's painful menstruation is a case in point (*Healing* pp. 128–131). Surgery and medicine had brought about improvement but scarcely a bearable relief. A redirection of her personal commitment in life, however, enabled her to achieve a reconciliation with her divorced mother. She was then asked to consider in her moments of meditation if her menstrual difficulties could be a physiological expression of rebellion against her lot, and it became clear to her that she was, in fact, refusing to accept her own womanliness. "I am never so pleased," she exclaimed, "as when people tell me that I ought to have been a boy (*Healing* p. 130). The acceptance of her femininity had far-reaching physiological effects and resulted in completely painless periods. It also changed her attitude toward other women, for by accepting her own sexuality, she was free to accept theirs. Others, it is true, have experienced similar changes in attitude without any conscious religious orientation, but this patient's change was born of "a longing to live at last the way God meant her to, as a woman, to act like a woman and to acquire a woman's gentleness and feminine qualities" (*Healing* p. 131).

A basic reorientation of life can bring with it a high degree of honest self-awareness. This, in Tournier's view, is what psychotherapeutic systems seek to achieve. They may differ in their understanding of persons and in their methods of helping, but if they are to be effective, they must have one thing in common—the honest interest, concern, and love of the helping person in relation to whom the patient can review his conflicts, seek new ways of resolving them, and adopt a new stance in life. Here a non-Christian helper can exhibit Christian virtues as well as a Christian. But the Christian therapist has one advantage: Beyond his skills and outward understanding, he may bring about a personal encounter between his patient and the living Christ. "The patient who has found Christ has found the source of power which will assure him of victory thereafter in every other circumstance of his life (*Healing* p. 249).

In proclaiming this sort of conviction, Tournier was not blind to the dangers of a formal, moralistic religion. He saw this influence to be harmful in the lives of many. He knew whereof he spoke in that he had experienced a strongly tinged Calvinistic nurture himself, but he also knew how different and how transforming his experience and his wife's had been when they entered the fellowship of the Oxford Group. "The moment Jesus Christ really comes into a person's life, he finds a new discipline, one which is no longer rigid, formalist, or heavy, but joyous, supple, and spontaneous" (*Healing* p. 189).

Such an experience presupposes that the person is relatively free from neurotic conflict. Tournier was the first to admit that to invite religion into a personality already manifesting psychological conflict was to invite disaster. "One cannot deny that there [can be] an inextricable mixture of authentic religious experience and psychical reactions of a definitely pathological nature" (*Healing* p. 274). In these circumstances, and in accordance with the principle of reciprocal causality, adequate psychological help would be needed to bring about appropriate change.

5

The meaning of the "medicine of the person," to which Tournier felt himself called as a result of rethinking his vocation, is a medicine "whose aim is the reformation of men's lives (*Healing* p. 203). Tournier would use his medical knowledge and skill where that was in order. For one patient he "prescribed physical exercises, gardening, rest, and a particular attention to her diet" (*Healing* p. 281). He would enable another to achieve that degree of self-awareness which any other competent psychotherapist would achieve. But for another his method was to start by "simply talking to her about Jesus Christ, about forgiveness, and about the peace that comes of giving oneself to him" (*Healing* p. 256).

Central to this kind of approach is, of course, the inner maturity of the physician himself which enables him to enter into that close personal relationship with his patient (involving mutual sharing), without which no radical healing of the person is possible. For Tournier this has meant a gladly embraced self-discipline undertaken to keep his own commitment directed steadily toward his rightful objective. "I have continued," he explains, "the practice of written meditation which [the Group] taught me, that attentive listening to what God is saying to us . . . in order to conduct our personal lives in accordance with his purpose" (*Healing* p. xiv).

4 ❖ Loneliness

In his day-to-day practice as a physician and counselor, Tournier was aware that the emotional isolation which we call loneliness is far commoner than we suppose and that it is frequently as painful as it is widespread. That his own past experience contributed to such recognition there can be no doubt, for he had known the sometimes unendurable bitterness of loneliness. "As a child, I was terribly withdrawn. Orphaned quite young, I withdrew into my own lonely little world, even though I was treated kindly. My daydreams and secret projects only isolated me more from the others. . . . I felt I was of no importance to anyone and that no one was really interested in me" (*Escape* p. 45).

In this respect, although for different reasons, Tournier resembled his compatriot C. G. Jung of Zurich. In recalling his early memories, dreams, and reflections, Jung owned that his entire youth was one of bitter loneliness, largely because of the dreams, images, and questions which arose within him and which he felt others did not know and did not even care to know.[1] When he later abandoned an academic career to devote himself to psychiatric practice and to a study of the unconscious, Jung experienced similar feelings. As an old man he confessed: "As a child I felt myself to be alone, and I am still, because I know things and must hint at things which others apparently know nothing of, and for the most part do not want to know. Loneliness does not come from having no people about one, but from being unable to communicate the things that seem important to oneself, or from holding certain views which others find inadmissible."[2]

These words are a reminder that solitude (being by oneself) and loneliness are not the same thing. One may be alone, or solitary, without feeling lonely. For example, in Wordsworth's "The Daffodils," the poet was alone as he lay on his couch quietly musing on the beauty of the daffodils he had seen,

> Beside the lake, beneath the trees,
> Fluttering and dancing in the breeze.

His solitude was not accompanied by feelings of loneliness. Indeed, he mentions, "the bliss of solitude" in the same poem. The poet was certainly alone but was not aware of isolation from others which gave him pain.

The felt isolation from others is the condition of loneliness about which Tournier was reflecting when he wrote *De La Solitude à la Communauté* (1943). The English version has been given the title *Escape from Loneliness*. As in so many of his books, Tournier did not aim at systematic exposition but rather "to express more extensively some of the insights into certain aspects of the problem, which I have gained through my daily work as a doctor" (*Escape* p. 87).

2

During our waking life our senses are subject to a continuous bombardment of light and sound, movement and color. We are unaware of much of this, except when we hear a particularly loud sound or see something especially colorful and beautiful. Experiments in this field has taught us that strange things happen when sensory input is reduced. We may hallucinate and become disoriented and so disturbed as to experience a temporary emotional disorder.[3]

If we can suffer from sensory deprivation, we can also suffer from emotional starvation. We need the love and support of others and find life unendurable if that kind of response is

reduced, limited, or withheld. As Tournier puts it, "There is
in the human heart an inexhaustible need to be loved and <
a continual fear of not being loved. Constantly, in all our
human relations and in all our activities, we look for proof
of love from the other person. We look for them as remedies
for our solitude. We seek others' reassurance" (*Escape* p. 133).

In that system of personality theory and therapeutic practice known as Transactional Analysis the term for this input
of human affection is "stroking."[4] Any signal of recognition, —
approval, or affection is a stroke, and we usually organize our
living in such a way as to receive a good number of strokes.
When we feel a little downcast or depressed, it usually means
that the stroke count is low.

Feelings of loneliness are related to the amount of stroking
we receive. Such feelings are marked among those who, for one
reason or another, are deprived of the emotional support they
normally experience. Thus, the ill, the infirm, the partner
abandoned by a mate, the widow, and those receiving institutional care, for example, are likely to experience feelings of
loneliness, some of them acute. The same is true for those who
move in their own small circle which contains little emotional
warmth. The religiously devout and those engaged in the
ecclesiastical structure as professionals may be victims of emotional isolation for this very reason. Such people, Tournier
noted, often tend to move in a world of their own where they
speak a language of their own and "in their passion for sin-
cerity part company with each other along a thousand different
ways" (*Escape* p. 22).

This is a topic on which Tournier felt obliged to write with
candor as well as sympathy: "I have rarely felt the modern
man's isolation more grippingly than in a certain deaconess
or in a certain pastor. . . . Among colleagues, they discuss
theology, church affairs, and sometimes even pastoral care, but
they practice no mutual pastoral care. They struggle alone with
their inextricable family problems, with their temptations,
with the guilt of their secret faults, never daring to unburden

themselves . . . because they are afraid of being condemned or of causing a scandal. . . . Even when doubt steals into their heart, they still have to preach, unless they dare to seek out a psychotherapeutic clinic in order once again to find themselves and to rebuild their faith, shattered by deceptions, disobediences, and loneliness" (*Escape* pp. 22, 23).

It is not only the invalid and those open to particular occupational hazards who are prone to feelings of loneliness. There are factors in our culture which open all of us to this kind of experience from time to time. Such factors are opposed to the creation of fellowship and consequently to that degree of emotional warmth which most of us need. The anonymity of large urban centers, the reduction of personal values in large business enterprises and in industry, the mobility of many families and the consequent lack of roots—these are some of the factors in our social surroundings that reduce the emotional input and thus expose us to painful feelings of loneliness.

3

Escape from Loneliness is largely an attempt to draw attention to some pressures in our culture which make the feeling of loneliness common to twentieth-century man. Tournier notes four areas in the mentality of our age which oppose the experience of fellowship and thus open the way to loneliness.

The first factor is what Tournier calls the parliamentary spirit. In a parliament or congress the members vie with one another in an attempt to further the sectional interests they represent. Their relations with other members are almost solely functional. "They never make contact with the other person deep down inside, but only with his outward role, his system of thought, his leanings, or his demands" (*Escape* p. 32).

Tournier was thinking about a family when he wrote these words, but he felt that such a family could represent society as a whole on a small scale. We accord a place to others, we respect their status, we recognize the importance of their distinctive function, but more often than not, we do not enjoy personal relations with them. "Each has his little trademark giving him the right to his little place in society. But it is a place, a function, a seat such as that of a congressman, and the man himself remains alone, without a personal relationship" (*Escape* p. 35).

The second characteristic of our culture which militates against the enjoyment of emotional closeness and thus predisposes us to feelings of loneliness is the spirit of independence. We do not refer to that personal autonomy and sense of responsibility which accompanies true freedom, but rather to that exaggerated assertiveness which claims only its own rights and makes its own way regardless of the consequences to others.

Tournier felt that one of the sources of this tendency is seen in the revolution in western thought associated with Descartes. "With Descartes, the individual has been made the first reality. He proves his own existence first of all . . . and then he approaches the study of the external world in terms of his own individual existence" (*Escape* p. 52). To attach importance to this particular individual or that was, indeed, to have significant consequences for the development of modern science and the empirical method; it was to have more far-reaching effects on the shape of human living when embodied in the sovereign claims of a nation-state and in the individualism of its citizens. Tournier, like any other counselor, was daily confronted with the unhappiness resulting from the conflicts of exaggerated, proud individualism. "Here is a husband who asserts his freedom in such a fashion as to deny the meaning of marriage: 'So long as I'm not unfaithful to my wife with other women, she has no say in my affairs' " (*Escape* p. 55).

The emancipation of women may be regarded as an extension of the same spirit of independence. These gains have been as wholesome as they were necessary; but some questions remain. "Her struggle for independence," notes Tournier, "ended in total victory. . . . Will she become intoxicated with independence, or will she bring to mankind a new quality of group experience? Sometimes the victors are victims of their own success" (*Escape* p. 67). The achievement of independence for women in the spheres of politics, economics, and sex has not been secured without cost. "Neurotic ailments break out whenever the soul is torn apart by conflicting forces. In women, there is an unrootable tendency towards submission, self-giving, and love. Yet our era inspires her toward self-sufficiency, self-direction, and insubmission" (*Escape* p. 75).

Closely associated with the spirit of independence but distinguishable from it is a third element, the spirit of possessiveness; the desire to "have" food, money and pleasure; the urge to "own" goods and things and persons; the striving to manage, manipulate, and dominate others. The disastrous consequences of this trend are no more clearly seen than in the institution of marriage and the family.

The desire to have one's pleasure, and to demand that one's mate supply it, is destructive of any appearance of marital love. Tournier writes very directly and to the point. "Every case of impotence in the man and of frigidity in the woman is closely tied with a wrong attitude towards physical love. The person is preoccupied with himself—with his success in sex and with the desired enjoyment. In this attitude there is self-analysis and fear of failure, which is enough to assure failure, and which in turn will bring self-preoccupation and self-pity" (*Escape* p. 90).

The love which dominates is, however, the most tragic form of possessiveness. When a mother's affection for her child takes this form, the outcome is disastrous. "Such love is, in fact, a terrible burden. Either the child is crushed by it and only vegetates, withdrawn and neurotic, and becoming his mother's despair, or else he openly rebels, to her complete consternation" (*Escape* p. 105). How different is true love which is disinterested, spontaneous, and pure. In contrast to dominating love, which demands that its object become completely dependent, there is pure love which "is to will the good for another" (*Escape* p. 115).

The fourth factor which Tournier regards as weakening our sense of community is the spirit of criticism, of jealousy, and of selfish demand. "The poor man envies the rich man for his money and comfort, while the rich man envies the carefree life he has lost. The spinster envies the married woman, and the childless woman envies the one who has the joy of motherhood. . . . Each thinks that the other's life is easier than his own" (*Escape* p. 117).

People may press their demands in a variety of ways. They may dedicate themselves to social uplift, parade their sufferings, take pride in being nonconformist, magnify their complaints, fasten on anyone inclined to show affection that they may show more—and all in the interests of receiving the affection for which they hunger. The pressure of keeping up the demand, however, is a tiring business, and those engaged in it become overly sensitive and lost in self pity. "They go from conflict to conflict, from catastrophe to catastrophe, and even though they always may be right, they nevertheless sow division and strife wherever they go" (*Escape* p. 145).

Tournier could see only one healing response for those who chose to dwell in grievances and live by demand. If such patterns of behavior are to be changed, they have to be met by acceptance, love, and forgiveness. "Forgiveness looks straight at the wrong, sees it in all its wrongness, and then forgives precisely because it is evil—just as God loves us because and in spite of our sin. . . ." (*Escape* p. 151). Forgiveness recognizes evil and injury for what they are, acknowledges the natural response of anger to them, and bears both before God.

4

Tournier's study of loneliness and escape from it consists largely in the recognition of those factors in our society that oppose the achievement of fellowship and thus increase our sensitivity to feelings of loneliness. His illustrations and case studies make it clear that some people are more vulnerable than others to feelings of loneliness. Indeed, their loneliness may be the result of their inability to relate satisfactorily to others. Thus, in any study of loneliness, we must bear in mind an individual's degree of vulnerability as well as factors in his cultural environment.

In a little work entitled *Le Secret* (1963), which appeared later in English as *Secrets,* Tournier noted that the capacity to have a secret and to keep it lies at the heart of personhood, at the center of individual formation. "Every human being needs secrecy in order to become himself and no longer only a member of his tribe" (*Secrets* p. 22).

He included this idea in his examination of loneliness. "What isolates the patient the most in his life—whether schoolboy, housewife, or worker—is the very thing that isolates us the most: our secrets" (*Escape* p. 44). When our secrets become overlaid with fear so that we cannot share them with others, our lines of communication are blocked, and we feel out of touch and lonely. We are involved in a condition of distance or separation from others; we cannot share with them our sense of "remorse for our wrongdoings, fears that haunt us, disgust with ourselves that we continually succumb to a certain recurring temptation, inner doubts . . . our jealousy and our anger, and even the naïve daydreams of glory by which we console ourselves" (*Escape* p. 45).

Such a condition is very common, and most people manage to live with a mild form of it. It is not easy for overly sensitive, vulnerable people to do so. Their sense of separation is even greater, and as a result, they experience a more painful degree of loneliness.

A vulnerable person is one whose sense of competence in living is impaired. He has little sense that he has the resources within himself to cope with the demands of life. Such a re-

duced sense of competence is now recognized to be evidence
of psychological damage sustained in the course of nurture. A
perceptive, short study, *Theory of Suicide by* M. L. Farber, ✓
analyzes the factors which bring about psychological damage,
three of which are more significant than others. The first is
"*A disruption in the symbiotic relationship between mother
and infant,*"[5] whereby the child suffers maternal deprivation
and becomes the victim of basic distrust rather than basic trust.
Second is *disparagement* which Farber describes as a virulent
destroyer of competence; "If a child is defined as helpless and
incompetent by his apparently omniscient parents, he can
hardly help but internalize their definition."[6] And third, the
induction of *guilt* by which many parents attempt to control a
child's aggression by making him feel that he has committed
unpardonable acts by virtue of which he must be basically
bad and worthless.

If a child is nurtured in this kind of atmosphere, his sense
of competence in human living most likely will be seriously
reduced. Lacking a sense of competence within himself, the
growing person is obliged to look outside himself, especially
to those nearest him, to supply what he lacks. He often becomes
an overly dependent person and is frequently disappointed in
the fulfillment of the demands he makes of others. "The feeling ⟨
of abandonment, of helplessness, of incompetence, generates
an unassuageable hunger for supplies of love, succorance,
goods, which—it is hoped—will provide strength and relief.
The demands are in the main made upon people close to the
subject—parents, spouses, lovers. These individuals cannot ⤺
supply what is demanded. Out of this frustration grows a great
rage against those who appear to refuse the demands."[7]

If vented, this rage would only destroy those who can supply
what is needed. Being contrary to the subject's values, its presence, though repressed, leaves him with a sense of guilt which,
in turn, adds to his already low self-esteem. It is difficult for
such a person to share with others the burden of anxiety and

guilt. He has been conditioned to feel basic distrust in his world. Inevitably he will feel emotionally isolated and lonely even in situations with people who are friendly to him.

This brings us back again to Tournier's *Secrets*. If the capacity to have and to keep a secret is a necessary part of human personhood, so also is the ability to share it with another. "If keeping a secret was the first step in the formation of the individual, telling it to a freely chosen confidant is going to constitute then the second step in the formation of the individual. . . . He who cannot keep a secret is not free. But he who can never reveal it is not free either" (*Secrets* p. 29). The way out of loneliness, then, is by way of sharing our secrets with someone we can trust. Hence understanding friends and the quality of the helping person is important in a therapeutic relationship.

We have mentioned that as a teen-ager Tournier rejoiced that his teacher Jules Dubois took an interest in him and his ideals and values. His marriage and family life broadened the way still further, and the fellowship he began to enjoy, as a result of his religious experience completed the deliverance. "True team life, in which complete trust in each man's conviction is the order . . . is nothing less than a revelation to the modern man. . . . To experience team life means that when there is a divergence of views, the problem is resolved by a common seeking for God's solution, undertaken in love and mutual loyalty. When I experienced this with friends from many lands and social backgrounds, and of many age groups and religious beliefs, I saw in the concept the social philosophy that our modern world so badly needs in order to get out of its individualism and its impersonalism, its formalism and its division" (*Escape* p. 184).

The fellowship of Tournier and his friends in the team owed itself to the spirit of Jesus. Only that "spirit can free [men] from formalism, independence, greed, and resentment, which stand in the way of the spirit of fellowship" (*Escape*

p. 189). The factors in our society which impede fellowship
and make for loneliness can thus be overcome by Christian experience. "Thus it is," he writes, "that Christian experience
first of all restores the human person and then spreads out
from person to person until it transforms society" (*Escape*
p. 163). Such a transformation is brought about as renewed
individuals discover their vocations and enter upon them.
It is vocation which unifies personal and social purposes. "In
the Christian's concept of society, the individual's relationship
to the larger community is seen in terms of vocation. Each
person accomplishes his life purpose to the degree in which
he fulfills the function to which God has called him, and to
the degree in which he does so according to the will of God.
Not only that, but society's purpose is fulfilled at the same
time" (*Escape* p. 168).

This assertion enabled Tournier once again to affirm the
importance of meditation as a means of discovering and preparing a man for his social role.

5 ❖ Fear

In du Maurier's novel, Rebecca was drowned in the bay.[1]
When the boat was recovered it was learned that the victim
herself had scuttled it. Only a short time before Rebecca's
physician had disclosed to her that she suffered from an in-
curable disease, and fearing the slow destruction of her life,
she had chosen to end it abruptly.

The pervasiveness of fear ranges from "a vague anxiety
which is all the more persistent because it has no precise object . . . to those more specific fears . . . of losing [a loved one]
. . . of loneliness . . . of responsibility . . . of hurting someone
. . . of being disappointed by reality . . . of success . . . of
failure" (*Strong and Weak* pp. 68–69). Fear of a lingering disease is only one of a host of fears which are present everywhere
but which are most noticeable in the lives of those whom the
physician seeks to help.

Tournier's experience as a doctor was not different from
that of his colleagues. He knew fear in himself, and he met it
universally in his patients. Indeed, almost all his work has
been devoted to little else but the relief of fear. "I often think
that my vocation, both in the field of psychology and in the
realm of the spirit, is nothing but the banishment of fear. . . .
If . . . I can be of help to others . . . it is because I have myself
learned to recognize my fears, and no longer lull myself with
the illusion that I can escape from them" (*Strong and Weak*
p. 94).

Tournier's book *The Strong and the Weak* is an essay on fear and the ways man reacts to it. It was written at a point in Tournier's life when he was particularly aware of his own fears. He and his wife had decided that they must leave the Oxford Group, a step which could only open them to the criticism of many whom they knew.

2

It is important to distinguish between fear and the temperamental factors which distinguish one person from another. Temperamental differences are, as we have already mentioned, a matter of terrain, of the person's psychosomatic make-up, and of his innate predisposition (cf. *Strong and Weak* p. 41). Such differences are, as William James points out, matched by differences in general attitude and philosophic outlook.[2]

If we bring two people into relationship with each other— one of whom is vigorous and confident; the other, quieter, more reticent, and obliged to direct his resources more carefully—it is apparent which will be dominant. In the give and take of life one will tend to conquer, the other will tend to yield. Tournier would ascribe the tendency to yield to genetic causes: "On the physical side a certain constitutional debility; on the psychological side a high coefficient of sensitivity and liability to emotional excitement" (*Strong and Weak* p. 42).

When these differing types of personality terrain become subject to accidental stresses in the course of nurture and development, a strong or weak reaction is added to the innate disposition. Two daughters may illustrate this point. The elder daughter of a possessive, domineering mother had become submissive, docile, and hesitant. Abandoning her own independence, she had become content to remain her mother's protegé and servant, but only at the cost of renouncing her own potential for adult love and sexuality. Her younger sister responded to the same tyranny by becoming a rebel. She had left home, had fended for herself, and not without suffering and heartbreak, had achieved success in her independent career. "She has become a strong woman," comments Tournier, "repressing every feeling of pity and imposing her will on all and sundry. She despises her sister . . . she dazzles a weak man who is seeking refuge in her strength. She marries him and crushes him in her turn" (*Strong and Weak* pp. 26–27). Between the two sisters there was more than a temperamental difference, though there was probably that too; there was a different response to the circumstances of their nurture and the accidental factors in their lives in which fear played an obviously significant part.

The circumstances in which fear is most likely to exert its powerful influence are, in Tournier's view, associated with parental discord and conflict (cf. *Strong and Weak* p. 45). The child becomes a victim of a destructive emotional climate. "He suffers doubly, for the hurt done by each of his parents to the other falls on him" (*Strong and Weak* p. 46). He becomes fearful lest another outbreak of passion occur. He is confused by the contradictory patterns which his parents present to him. For example, he may find that his father tends to abdicate his parental role, while his mother, unhappy in her relationship with her husband, dominates him. "The father holds aloof from the child, taking no further interest in him because he has become the private property of the mother. He leaves him defenseless in face of what amounts to emotional blackmail by his mother, who dominates the child with her arbitrary demands and her tears" (*Strong and Weak* p. 47).

This emotional domination becomes for the child a deprivation of true affection because his mother "loves him not for himself but selfishly, for her own satisfaction" (*Strong and Weak* p. 48). She becomes overly solicitous and demanding, breeding in her child a sense of having to reach a standard which he never can achieve, therefore causing an exaggerated feeling of guilt for his failure to do so. Exposed to this kind of situation one child, so disposed by temperament and disposition, will respond with fearfulness; another, of a more vigorous and more vital nature, will respond boldly. The one, to use Tournier's language, will present to life an appearance of weakness, the other an appearance of strength.

3

Those who seem weak and those who seem strong differ only in appearance; in reality they are alike for they are both responding to basic fear. The weak are self-conscious, self-depreciating, easily flustered, escapist, prone to despair and depression, overly ready to withdraw from the struggle of life (cf. *Strong and Weak* p. 97). "The weak person is unable quickly to throw off the effects of an annoyance, a disagreeable suggestion, or a failure" (*Strong and Weak* p. 100). He is hesitant in the face of the choices before him, and he needs more time and tranquility to make up his mind. Under pressure, he is likely to manifest signs of exhaustion. "Fatigue," notes Tournier, "is the weak reaction par excellence, the eclipse of a person's strength when he comes up against an unsurmountable obstacle" (*Strong and Weak* p. 101).

This situation is rarely caused by overwork but more frequently by excess of zeal, especially when the person attempts to dull the pain of conflict with a whirl of feverish activity (cf. *Strong and Weak* p. 103). But it is rebellion which is the main source of fatigue. "A man who is discontented in his work, who does it only with a continual inner irritation, who blames circumstances or other people for having unjustly imposed on him a task that is beyond his strength . . . such a man is worn out with fatigue" (*Strong and Weak* p. 105).

A strike reaction is another form by which weakness shows itself. The lazy person is usually one who is on strike and "what is needed is to find out what has injured him rather than to rebuke him. The passivity shown by many people is another form of strike reaction, while petty time-wasting and much of our forgetfulness is to be seen as a sort of go-slow strike" (*Strong and Weak* pp. 107–108).

The weak response to life which fear may cause is seen most clearly in the neurotic, who is unhappy and exhibits certain specific symptoms, overwhelming fears, depressions, and impeded organic functions. He is not efficient in the living process. His feelings of security and self-esteem are disturbed; his ability to relate himself to others in satisfying ways is diminished. Lonely and fearful, he cannot understand himself since he has no insight into his condition. Yet he knows that the time is out of joint and he with it. It is now known that fear plays a crucial part in the formation of such conditions.

The newborn child needs a warm, intimate, and continuous relationship of a satisfying and enjoyable sort with his mother, or with some other significant person who offers him mothering attention. "The child needs to feel he is an object of pleasure and pride to his mother; the mother needs to feel an expansion of her own personality in the personality of her child; each needs to feel closely identified with the other."[3]

In this relationship the mother meets a biological and psychological need of the child and her care reaches him by means of his own body. Such a relationship is the child's first sensuous experience of life, and if satisfactory, becomes the gateway to the more complex relationships of the growing self in its environment.

Suppose, however, that the child, for whatever reason, feels neglected, rejected, and disapproved. The first reaction of the child to feelings of rejection will be a combination of terror, rage, and hate; rage for being frustrated in his need for gratification; hatred because he must continue to press his demands on a denying object if he is to survive; and terror because his whole experience is a threat to life itself.

Because of the unitary nature of the child, emotional reactions occur in a field in which body-mind components combine. Bodily functions may be inhibited insofar as fear of any kind is an inhibiting emotion. The overwhelming fear, being so painful an emotion, must be somehow obliterated. Here the mechanism of repression begins to operate—that automatic inhibition of part of the self by another part.

Denied love in reality but still in need of it, the child may either retreat from the struggle and seek to comfort himself, that is, may relapse into a primitive form of self-pity, or he may seek consolation and pleasure in his own body by becoming autoerotic. Or he may become entirely independent and set out to achive mastery by becoming aggressive.

Tournier calls this last procedure the strong reaction. He noticed it in himself: "Though I never admitted it to myself," he writes, "I was terribly lonely; I was afraid of other people. Then I perceived that my aptitude for handling, formulating, and defending ideas could be used as an admission ticket to society. I could thus win the affection and esteem for which I craved in order to bolster up my self-confidence. I played the card. I wrote plays, I mugged up mathematics, studied law . . . became president of my students' union . . . and passed my medical examinations with flying colors" (*Strong and Weak* p. 131).

But it was all a psychological compensation (reaction forma- — tion) for feelings of inferiority born of fear. He was exemplifying the Adlerian principle that the will to power is a compensating mechanism for organic or personal inferiority which the individual can never have without being secretly afraid.

Tournier lists examples of these compensating forms of behavior: retaliation, vengeance, criticism, bluster, the affectation of nonconformity in dress and manner, loquacity, and the proselytizing spirit of some religious people.

He summarizes: "The strong reaction is to give ourselves an appearance of assurance and aggressiveness in order to hide our weakness, to cover up our own fear by inspiring fear in others, to parade our virtues in order to cloak our vices" (*Strong and Weak* p. 22).

"So, then, there are not, as the world thinks, weak persons

on the one hand, and on the other the strong. There are, on
the one hand, weak persons who are aware of their weakness
. . . and there are on the other hand weak persons who believe
in the value of their strong reactions, of their doctrines, their
successes, and their virtues" (*Strong and Weak* p. 176).

4

A tragedy befalls both the person who responds to fear with
obvious weakness and the person who reacts with apparent
strength. Both find a solution to their problems but only at
the expense of excluding part of their personality from the
stream of growth and development. The weak repress their
native assertiveness, and the strong repress their gentleness and
tenderness. "All the symptoms shown by neurotics, all that we
have called weak reactions, they [the Freudians] believe to stem
from the repression of their natural aggressiveness, of the will
to live, of the individual's need to expand, of his libido"
(*Strong and Weak* p. 179).

There are some Christians who believe that meek submission
to injustice, the curbing of natural desire, and self-abnegation
in respect of ambition are what their faith prescribes. They
claim Christian support for the weak reaction, citing such
passages as, "Do not set yourself against the man who wrongs
you. If someone slaps you on the right cheek, turn and offer
him your left. If a man wants to sue you for your shirt, let him
have your coat as well" (Matt. 5:39, NEB).

Tournier believes that, wrongly interpreted, this may lead
to dangerous error. "There is all the difference in the world
between the strong man, capable of defending himself, who
renounces that power in order to follow Christ and obey God,
and the man who does not dare to defend himself, who is
afraid, and who weakly gives way" (*Strong and Weak* pp.
182–183).

Submissiveness born of fear is one thing; the courage which

springs from the renunciation of strength is something quite
different. "There is," affirms Tournier, "a legitimate defense
of the person founded on the biblical revelation, and . . . to
repress this legitimate defense is to disobey God and not to
practice Christian nonresistance" (*Strong and Weak* p. 184).

Personal fulfillment can only be achieved if the weak gear
their native assertiveness to the requirements of their living
and if the strong allow their natural gentleness (a characteristic
of every potential parent) to soften and enrich their character.
In Tournier's experience the way to achieve this is by means
of meditation. "Prayer will not deliver us from our natural reactions, whether weak or strong; but it will bring us to recognize them for what they are, and thus continually to fresh
experiences of grace" (*Strong and Weak* p. 150).

Most people would agree that all forms of therapy aim at
bringing about, among other things, an increase in the person's
self-awareness. Psychoanalysis, various forms of psychotherapy,
group therapy, encounter or sensitivity groups certainly achieve
this purpose to a greater or lesser extent. Tournier would,
doubtless, agree with this, but for him, the moment of self-
awareness par excellence occurs in the presence of God. What
he has written as a general principle in the third person, could
well have been written as a particular truth in the first.

"And in meditation before God he learns to distinguish
whether the passion that has carried him away is no more
than a strong reaction which it is God's will that he should
overcome; or whether the renunciation which he has in mind
is no more than a weak reaction which God is calling him to
overcome; whether the forgiveness he had offered is genuine
or not; whether his readiness to fight is legitimate or not"
(*Strong and Weak* p. 189).

Is the benefit Tournier receives in meditation then to be
equated with that which a person receives from therapeutic
sessions? Tournier repudiates this suggestion because he believes in a transcendent God, that is, in a Creator who must

not be confused with the life forces and the energies at work in his own creation.

"There are two motive powers at work in the mind: instinct and the Holy Spirit. Psychology seeks to liberate natural strength, the libido, instinct; and that is legitimate and salutary. But we who are believers seek, over and above that, to tap a new source of power for man, the supernatural strength which comes from the Holy Spirit; it is a different strength, which does not go against that of instinct, but which goes beyond it, controlling and directing it, so that man may pass from mere animal life into the life of the person. . . . The strength which comes from God can heal, it can give strength to the weak, but that is only one aspect of its power. It does much more; it saves and quickens. Salvation and healing do not coincide. Healing may be a sign of salvation, but salvation goes far beyond healing, because it is needed by the healthy and strong as much as by the weak and the sick" (*Strong and Weak* pp. 236, 238).

6 ❖ The Meaning of Persons

The underlying philosophy of the medicine of the person can be put quite simply: If you would heal another, treat him in his entirety. You should take his medical history, examine his body, question him, and try to reach an understanding of his complaint on that basis. You should also estimate his psychological make-up, attempt to gauge the degree of conflict within him, appreciate his characteristic responses, study his coping resources, and test the measurable aspects of his personality. But neither of these approaches, either together or singly, will disclose the essential being of the person before you. Such observations do not reveal him, although they may yield much information about him.

"Life, the Spirit, the person, are not substantial realities which we can hold in our hands. They cannot be docketed, analyzed, or described. They are as fleeting as a lightning flash —by the time we have seen their light and heard the rumbling that follows them, they have already gone. We cannot reach the person either by means of introspection or by objective scientific study" (*Meaning* p. 119).

It is in the moment of communion that personal knowledge occurs. "Through information I can understand a case; only through communion shall I be able to understand a person" (*Meaning* p. 25). In such moments of communion a situation is created in which our separateness is overcome and we begin to be healed, for, if you think of it, every ailment we have, whether physical, social, or personal, is a kind of alienation or separation from our true being.

Given such an approach, it is easy to see why Tournier became preoccupied with the meaning of persons. What is a person? Who am I? Why is it that there are inherently different types of personality? What light does the Bible shed on our understanding of persons? What is required if a person is to become fully human and to display his characteristic creativity? What are the special poignancies of human living? What are the conditions of happiness in marriage, in society, or elsewhere? Here we shall glance at the first question only, What is a person?

2

Individuality, rationality, and self-awareness are the characteristics of persons that have been underlined in many classical definitions of personality. Boethius (c. A.D. 480–524), for example, said that "a person is an individual substance of a rational nature" (*Persona est substantia individua rationalis naturae*). Thus he stressed the uniqueness, the unexchangeable nature of a person, and drew attention to a person's capacity to reason, to infer, to deal with concepts, and to appreciate the logic of an argument.

In describing man as "a thinking, intelligent being, that has reason and reflection and considers itself as itself, the same thinking thing in different times and places" John Locke (1632–1704) urged that we must add self-awareness and continuity to rationality when we talk of persons.[1]

Individuality, rationality, and self-awareness are indeed inseparable factors from the person. Tournier would never have been satisfied with this definition, for from his point of view, there is something indefinable and mysterious about the core of a person. "The person always eludes our grasp; it is never static. It refuses to be confined within concepts, formulae, and definitions. It is not a thing to be encompassed, but a point of attraction, a guiding force, a direction, an attitude, which demands from us a corresponding attitude, which moves us to action and commits us" (*Meaning* p. 179). Here the person is seen to be someone who is capable of communing with another, who exercises choices for which he makes himself responsible, and who can make commitments to others, to life itself, and to that which transcends life.

Tournier recalls the remarkable experience of meeting a man who had formerly been an opponent and an adversary. "Here he was opening his heart to me. I too opened mine to him. He had come to talk to me about his personal life and his sufferings. I was making the discovery of his person . . . his secrets, his solitude, his feelings. . . . I talked with him about my own personal experiences, and realized that this former adversary had the same needs and the same difficulties as I, the same longing to find life and fellowship again" (*Meaning* p. 181).

This was a moment of transparency when two persons communed. In Tournier's experience such moments are also moments of healing.

"Those who helped me most to free myself from the complex I had as a result of being an orphan, which kept me reserved and unsociable until after the age of thirty, and which blocked for me the road to personal contact, were not doctors, much less specialists. They were my wife and those of my friends who . . . were frank and open with me" (*Meaning* pp. 135–136).

Such dialogue, however, does not occur as frequently and as readily as it ought. Of the reasons that could be given for this, perhaps the most fundamental is that the person is often hidden behind what Tournier calls the personage. Our interaction with another is more often with the phenomena he presents to us than with the self underlying the appearance. Perhaps the following outline may make this point more clearly.

3

There is at the heart of every man a central core of self from which spring his creativity, his choices, and his commitment. Its point is marked by the pronoun "I." Here lies the source of a man's freedom and responsibility; here is to be found the mystery of his person. In virtue of this inner core he enjoys a certain unity, continuity, and uniqueness in the adventure of living, for he can see life and feel about his past in his own distinctive way. "The person is a potential, a current of life which surges up continually and which manifests itself in a fresh light at every new blossoming forth of life" (*Meaning* p. 232).

This inner, mysterious core is to the whole man as the conductor is to an orchestra, but, unlike the conductor, it cannot be observed or measured. It can only be known as it discloses itself in dialogue with another, as it affirms itself in authentic choice, and as it fulfills itself in final commitment to those values which are held to be ultimate (cf. *Meaning* p. 233).

In deep and sincere conversation with a patient, Tournier finds that "there suddenly awakens within me the certainty that I am no longer learning, but understanding. . . . It is not the sum of what I have learned. It is a light which has suddenly burst forth from our personal contact. . . . [This] intuitive understanding, . . . the personal contact which my patient and I both experienced at once and which awakened in us the certainty that we understood each other, seems at first sight to be much more subjective, since it is no longer scientific. And that is why it is much more independent of whatever psychological theories each of us may have" (*Meaning* pp. 22–23).

In the normal course of life, however, it is not the person of another which is most apparent. The phenomena associated with him are much more apparent, that is, his physique, gestures, prevailing moods, and the role he plays in society. These phenomena help to frame an image, and it is to this image that others respond. In other words, one is usually more concerned with the appearance of the man than with the reality.

When Tournier speaks of the personage, as distinct from the person, he is referring to what we have just called the appearance of the man. "There is thus a strange relationship between the personage and the person," he adds, "they are linked together, and yet they remain distinct. I can approach the person only through that image which at one and the same time allows me glimpses of it and also tends to hide it from me, reveals as well as conceals it" (*Meaning* p. 15).

In the course of nurture and education, whereby we are shaped to play a certain role in our culture, there is built up in us a set of responses, habits, and skills which qualify us to fulfill our role but which modify the expression of ourselves as persons. "Education is not merely an external constraint. It insinuates itself into the very core of the child's being. There it sets up powerful reflexes. The result is that an inner conflict takes place between the spontaneous nature which cannot be destroyed, and these reflexes which prevent it from manifesting itself. This conflict paralyzes spontaneous expression, canceling out the two opposing forces" (*Meaning* p. 48).

A patient once related to Tournier that he was several times on the point of doing some daring act. He felt that an immense potential of audacity was boiling up within him. He was frightened and automatically the brake implanted within him by his mother was applied (cf. *Meaning* p. 48). He was inhibited by his personage. We become prisoners of the personage, and our life becomes a scene of continuing conflict which may declare itself not only in emotional unrest but in physical illness. The origins of the conflict may be noted more precisely when we recognize the powerful influence which is exerted on a child through the fear of the loss of his parents' love. This fear will oblige him to conform to their wishes; a pattern of behavior is formed within him and thus his personage begins to take shape.

A child, for example, might wish to go out into the streets to play with his comrades and to dress as they do, only to be told: "Boys of our class don't roam the streets in company with urchins" (*Meaning* p. 19). Fearing the consequences of rejecting his parents' wishes, he does not go out to play. As such experiences are repeated, there is built up within him a self-image which excludes from itself the idea of playing in the streets. Further, impulses which prompt him to play in the streets are regarded as bad and are therefore excluded from awareness. His personage does not contain this element of play within it, though in the depths of his person the impulses remain.

Carl Rogers's theory of personality includes a distinction similar to that which Tournier makes between the personage and the person. Rogers speaks on the one hand of the phenomenal or experiential field, at the center of which stands the individual, and on the other, of its self-structure. "*As a result of interaction with the environment, and particularly as a result of evaluational interaction with others, the structure of self is formed.*"[2] Because the child's perception of himself as lovable and worthy of love is a core element in his self-experience, he will behave in such a way as to preserve that core and will value his experience "in terms of the attitudes held by his parents or by others who are in intimate association with him."[3] At the same time he will deny awareness of those impulses which conflict with the expectations of others.

Although conformity to the requirements of society is necessary if children are to be socialized, the demand may be so heavy and be made at such an early stage in life that the child's natural growth is disrupted. He is obliged to abandon his native, spontaneous striving for a socially acceptable mode of behavior which denies a good part of the reality within him. Thus, when he grows up, he may, for example, feel obliged to forsake a fiancée because that is what his mother demands. "A young student came to see me," Tournier records. "He too had hesitated between his mother and his fiancée. In spite of misgivings, he had given up seeing his fiancée, or at least had only seen her in secret, in order to appease his mother, and since that time he had suffered from all kinds of odd illnesses. 'Is that your aim in life,' I asked him 'to live for your mother?' " (*Meaning* p. 200). Apparently this had been this student's aim up to that moment. The vital center of his personal striving had long since become submissive to a false structure, or personage, which had at all costs to preserve the regard of his mother.

It is when the conflict between the person and the personage is acute that the individual is said to suffer from emotional disorder and its accompanying unhappiness. Yet it is a conflict from which none of us is free. If we differ from one another it is in degree, not in kind. Tournier knew this from his own experience, and that is why we find him citing so approvingly an important study by Henri Bergson, *The Two Sources of Morality and Religion*. "A substantial half of our morality," Bergson noted, "includes duties whose obligatory character is to be explained fundamentally by the pressure of society on the individual. . . . The rest of morality expresses a certain emotional state, [for] actually we yield not to a pressure but to an attraction. . . ."[4]

4

This restriction of the person by the personage may achieve social conformity, but it does not take place without harm to the unique qualities of the person. We noted earlier that such unique qualities are in the individual's capacity for communion in dialogue, for responsible choices, and for commitment. It is these precious capacities that are harmed. For example, the unique occasion of dialogue between partners in marriage may frequently be missed. "One will dominate the other, and there will no longer be a dialogue because one of the persons is eclipsed, his power of self-determination paralyzed" (*Meaning* p. 137). Or transparency, which is both the openness through which one can see to the depths of another and the candour which expresses that depth, may be blurred when the partners begin to calculate what they will say or not say (cf. *Meaning* p. 138).

Responsible choice is another victim of this conflict. Some lives manifest a steady avoidance of responsibility; their characteristic reply to any invitation that they meet such a demand is negative. They prefer that someone else shoulder the burden of choice, whether that be a professional superior or a marital partner.

Commitment calls for true self-affirmation, a process which is reduced in strength wherever the person is dominated by the personage. Again, marriage provides the best illustration, for it presents to persons the temptation to replace the moral dialogue by sexual interaction. "They evade the difficult encounter of personalities . . . by taking the easy road of physical love" (*Meaning* p. 139). It is at this point that Tournier sees the danger of premarital sexual intercourse. When divorced from the context of commitment and faithfulness, sex is apt to go bad.

There are other ways, of course, of viewing the harm done to the person by a dominating personage. Tournier, for example, fully accepts the Freudian view that sexuality is a function of the total person and therefore expects to find disorders of the sexual function where there are conflicts within the personality. "An impotent man perceives that his infirmity is but a mask to hide a temperament so potent that he is afraid of it; and then that the indifference he now feels with regard to women is a second mask, hiding the first" (*Meaning* p. 59). Or, still within the Freudian framework, Tournier notes that the restricted person exhibits a reduced capacity for assertiveness (the creative use of aggression).

Tournier finds much unfulfilled potential in the life where —
the personage holds sway and feels that the Bible confirms
this finding. Many of the dreams recorded in the Scriptures,
for example, are forward-looking and represent the fulfillment
of the personal aspiration which has been unfulfilled or denied
in real life. This is in line with "Jung's studies on the pur-
posive nature of dreams, taking them as an expression of the
aspirations of men's souls" (*Casebook* p. 73).

In general, it may be said that the man who experiences
too severe a conflict between his person and his personage is —
robbed of the energies he needs for living courageously and
adventurously. He remains an infant at heart because he has
not been free to become an adult. As one of Tournier's patients
remarked, "All my reactions are those of a child, but I have to
hide them behind a personage which acts and speaks like a
grown-up" (*Meaning* p. 82). If the patient could be helped to
leap over the walls of the personage which hem him in, he
could become adult; his native potential could be set free for
the adventure of living. Tournier sees this as precisely the
doctor's task. "The task of the doctor is to help each of his —
patients to become a person, to assume his proper responsibilities" (*Meaning* p. 203).

5

Tournier himself was for many years the victim of his personage, but later he was to discover that his personage was
less oppressive than he might have expected. In fact, he came
to accept it as an expressive part of his make-up. But in the
beginning he was a victim. The loss of his parents at an early
age left him reserved, timid, and unsociable. "When I was a
child, submerged in my 'orphan complex,' I was very reserved
with my comrades; I preferred the companionship of my dog.
. . . It was to him that I told my secrets . . ." (*Meaning* p. 128).

He began to find himself liberated as he entered into dialogue with others and with God. Indeed, dialogue is not only the means whereby the person is known; it is the way par excellence whereby he is healed. If you relate to him in a warm, understanding way, give him time, hear his story, let him say where the shoe pinches, and indicate what steps he has taken to cope with his difficulty, a friendly interchange will begin, especially if, in addition to giving him the benefit of whatever knowledge and skill you have, you share something of yourself with him. If there is genuine mutuality in this conversation, personal knowledge will grow and with it will come healing. "The people who have helped me most are . . . those who have listened to me in silence, and then told me of their own personal life, their own difficulties and experiences. It is this give and take that makes the dialogue" (*Meaning* p. 191).[5]

Dialogue helps to bring a man into accord with himself; it enables him to become what he potentially is. It redirects his gaze from himself to others, to the wider responsibilities of life, and to God.

You might imagine that one would readily welcome so beneficial a situation. However, while one needs to enter into dialogue, he also seeks to escape it. He resists the invitation to dialogue because he is afraid to know himself and the feelings that are inseparable from any healthy self-knowledge (cf. *Meaning* pp. 152–153). He fears, too, the memory of the things for which he knows he is responsible and which arouse a sense of guilt.

Only absolute honesty and fearless confession in the dialogue relationship will remedy ills. "A bad conscience can, over a period of years, so strangle a person's life that his physical and psychical powers of resistance are thereby impaired. It can be the root cause of certain psychosomatic affections. It is like a stopper which can be pulled out by confession, so that life begins at once to flow again" (*Meaning* p. 157).

It follows that the quality of the dialogue relationship is of profound importance. "When we are aiming at practicing a whole medicine, a medicine of the person, which will help the patient to live, and awaken the forces of life within him, the important thing is . . . the personal bond between him and ourselves. We ourselves are involved; we exercise a personal influence upon the patient" (*Casebook* pp. 236–237).

If honesty is required on the part of the one who confesses, integrity is needed on the part of the helping person. The one in need of healing has to find in his helper, not only wide knowledge and technical skill, but a rich and wholesome human person. "Psychological health," notes Tournier, "is as important to the practice of medicine as medical knowledge" (*Casebook* p. 211).

6

We have returned, once again, to the question of healing, the physiological and psychosocial aspects of which have now received some attention. But man, in the thought of Tournier, lives his life in a context wider than that indicated by his body and his place in culture and society. Nature and history are two vitally important dimensions, but they have to be considered in relation to that of Spirit.

In *The Meaning of Persons* Tournier notes that *sarx* (flesh) in the Pauline vocabulary denotes man in his disorder, while *pneuma* (spirit) denotes man renewed. The first speaks of the total man disrupted; the second of the total man restored to fellowship with God.

In an earlier work, *A Doctor's Casebook in the Light of the Bible,* Tournier had devoted careful thought to the context of man's life as it is indicated in the Bible and in particular to the idea that meaning attaches to things and occurrences insofar as they have a positive or negative relation to God. "With God, everything takes on meaning, everything has value, either positive or negative" (*Casebook* p. 34). Human nature and life in its disorder stands in negative relation to God; as positively related, it is healed and restored.

Tournier sees disease and death as signs of man's disordered condition, while healing and renewal are signs of God's gracious activity. In this life both disease and healing are partial and preliminary. Disease points to the end of man in death; healing is a stay of execution, a respite from the inevitable outcome. "Healing is an effect and a sign of God's mercy, extending the term of our life" (*Casebook* p. 215). Thus medicine is a means of collaborating with the Creator in achieving his purposes. It is a means of helping men to live as persons; it is also a means of directing their steps toward death. "That seems to me to sum up the whole of medicine—helping men to live and to die" (*Casebook* p. 179).

It is difficult to imagine anyone helping another to accept the inevitability of death without faith in the God who is above death and who holds in his hands the gift of resurrection. "When science has done all it can do, when the doctor is . . . accompanying his patient to the gates of death, this inner conviction of the certainty of resurrection is the only true consolation that remains" (*Casebook* p. 220).

The hope of resurrection and of the final vision of God, in Tournier's view, is inseparable from a living faith in the risen Christ now. Indeed, faith of this sort is, for him, the highest good, certainly higher than health.

Meeting an old pastor one day, Tournier was impressed by the vitality of his faith in Jesus, an experience which prompted him and his wife to seek the same thing for themselves. "Since then He has been the center of my devotion and my traveling companion. . . . He is a friend with whom I can discuss everything that happens in my life. He shares my joy and my pain, my hopes and fears. He is there when a patient speaks to me from his heart, listening to him with me and better than I can. And when the patient has gone I can talk to Him about it" (*Casebook* p. 237).

Since, for Tournier, this is the highest good it enables him to assume a detached attitude towards illness and death. "In order for affliction to be borne patiently, it is clear that a certain spirit of detachment, from oneself and from worry about one's health, as well as from life itself, is necessary. Only a person who has come to know that the highest good is fellowship with Jesus can aspire to such detachment" (*Casebook* p. 242).

Tournier's general understanding of the meaning of persons can be expressed in terms of what they have been given, of what they have become, their response to the gift and to the becoming, the degree of conflict which they exhibit, and the means and degree of their healing. It is now time to turn to another of the more poignant human experiences, that of guilt.

7 ❖ Guilt

"There is no life without conflict; no conflict without guilt" (*Guilt and Grace* p. 75). In this terse statement Tournier points to the universality of guilt in human life. Guilt is so much a part of man's condition that any discipline which studies life and behavior must be concerned with it. It is a religious problem that interests the theologian, a social problem that interests the sociologist, and a psychological problem that interests the psychologist. Above all, "it is a human problem, a form of suffering peculiar to man" (*Guilt and Grace* p. 213), and it is therefore a concern of every man, not least of those who reflect creatively on the human condition and who express that reflection in literature and art.

Having said that guilt is central in man's experience, Tournier is careful to add that "life is something which is borne and felt rather than thought" (*Guilt and Grace* p. 92). In other words, guilt is primarily an affective state; it is something we feel. As we shall see later, guilt may also be a state of affairs, but that aspect of guilt which we find painful is its felt aspect. If we remember this, we shall avoid the serious error of imagining that the problem of guilt can be handled as an intellectual exercise.

In the presence of any painful affect we find ourselves doing one of two things; and sometimes we try to do them both at the same time. We can erect *defenses* against the affect so as to reduce its painfulness, or we may muster what resources we can to *cope* with it. To the questions of defense and of coping we shall return later. For the moment we must pause to occupy ourselves with the many faces of guilt and attend to some distinctions within the concept of guilt.

It is in outlining the varieties of guilt situations and experiences that Tournier's anecdotal approach comes into its own. Philosophers may content themselves with generalities, but the doctor has to concern himself with cases, with this particular instance of guilt or that. Tournier is no exception; he stresses the particular.

A child, for example, may feel that he is guilty of the death of a parent, brother or sister; a single woman may feel guilty for not being married; a sick person may feel guilty for being ill and for being a burden to others. Tournier himself felt guilty for neglecting to cultivate a friendship, and equally guilty for the forced camaraderie he assumed in order to cover his neglect. Unanswered letters on his desk and unread journals on his bookshelf also pointed the accusing finger at him and made him feel guilty (*Guilt and Grace* pp. 18, 21, 25, 28).

The doctor who sends a bill when his patient is no better; those who earn too much too easily; the person who neglects to perform a good within his power; the parent who worries over a child's late return from school; the man who does not achieve a goal to which he has aspired; the doctor confronted by a dead patient—all are victims of guilt feelings.

With an eye to himself and to others, Tournier makes the short, sharp comment that "all inferiority is experienced as guilt" (*Guilt and Grace* p. 24). This does not identify feelings of inferiority with feelings of guilt; it merely suggests that whenever a man feels inferior, a feeling of guilt may be detected not very far away.

2

Passing now to note some distinctions within the concept of guilt, we must allow that we can be guilty without feeling guilty. With his customary candor Tournier cites an example from his own experience: "While I was preparing this study I suddenly received a telegram from America. I had promised to send an article for the month already passed, and there was the periodical in which it was to appear ready for printing! I had completely forgotten" (*Guilt and Grace* p. 42). That moment of embarrassment brought to him a feeling of guilt, but prior to it, though still guilty of forgetfulness, he had felt nothing.

Some friends and I, let us say, visit a river pool in order to bathe. I know the spot well and can judge precisely just where one can dive into the water with safety. Running easily down the slope, which ends abruptly at the edge of some ground overhanging the pool by several feet, I take a header into the water. A visitor immediately follows my example but he is unaware of the exact point for safe entry. He makes his dive slightly to the left of mine and in a different direction. He lands in shallower water, strikes his head on the bottom, and is taken from the pool seriously injured. I learn later that he has become a paraplegic for life.

Between the time of his dive and the discovery of his condition, I might feel a sense of deep regret that a friend had sustained an unfortunate injury, but hardly a sense of guilt for the state of affairs which my own action had brought about. When the real nature of his injury is disclosed, I shall probably feel an acute sense of guilt. I had plunged thoughtlessly into the water without giving him warning. By following my example and without possessing my exact knowledge, a young man had been injured for life. I was guilty of helping to bring about this state of affairs before I felt guilty for doing so. Thus, guilt as a state of affairs has to be distinguished from a feeling of guilt.[1]

A further distinction has to be noted within the felt aspect of guilt. Some guilt feeling is *true*, that is, appropriate in the circumstances of its occurrence. Tournier mentions, for example, "the keen sense of guilt which an abortion always occasions either in the case of an unmarried woman or a married woman, or else in the case of the lover or the husband or even the parents-in-law who have often forced the woman to undergo abortion. There enters into it, certainly, the guilty conscience of an attempt against life, but the feeling of guilt is usually more keenly felt as the shame of having committed a cowardly act (*Guilt and Grace* p. 56). Such guilt feeling is appropriate in the circumstances; it is realistic and true.

A person may feel guilty without being so. His feeling may be inappropriate; it may be unrealistic, exaggerated, and *false*. On his first day at school Tournier found himself to be the only child wearing a wide-brimmed hat, a circumstance which earned him a nickname and much ribald reproach. "This affected me deeply; I was an orphan and withdrawn and was here having my first experience of that pitiless society of a school class. . . . I felt ashamed and guilty at not being like the others" (*Guilt and Grace* p. 33). This response may be understandable but it is also unrealistic. Why should a boy feel guilty for wearing a certain kind of hat? The circumstances did not warrant the feeling.

It is this distinction between true and false feelings of guilt that provided the central focus for Tournier's careful study *Guilt and Grace*. The French title, *Vraie ou Fausse Culpabilité*, leaves no doubt of this fact.

Why should we be the victims of true and false feelings of guilt? The simple answer is that we have not sufficiently grown up. It is the survival of infantile forms of response that make us victims of unrealistic and exaggerated feelings of guilt. We may understand something of the way in which this comes about if we note the following argument.

Every normal child is endowed at birth with a certain constitution and characteristic potentialities and propensities which, if rightly nurtured, will permit him to develop a genuine self, uniquely and authentically his. There are, moreover, certain innate trends in the newborn infant which move him in the direction of (*toward*) other people because he needs them if he is to be human at all. There are others which impel him to move *against* other people when they frustrate him or oppose his own good, and there are others which oblige him to *move away* from other people in search of his own independence and achievement.

Karen Horney (1885–1952), who first suggested this way of putting things, has emphasized her meaning as follows: "When moving *toward* people he accepts his own helplessness, and in spite of estrangement and fears tries to win the affection of others and to lean on them. Only in this way can he feel safe with them. When he moves *against* people he accepts and takes for granted the hostility around him, and determines consciously or unconsciously, to fight. . . . When he moves *away from* people he wants neither to belong nor to fight, but keeps apart."[2]

The healthy individual has, after all, to assert himself against others in a competitive world; he has to be able to be detached from them in the interests of his own integrity and yet be capable of wholesome dependence upon others. True selfhood will include a harmonious blend of these trends.

For this blending to occur the child requires an attitude of warm acceptance, sympathetic understanding, and wise guidance. If he meets rejection, intolerance, and suspicion, if those who nurture him are overdemanding, overindulgent, intimidating, or erratic in their behavior toward him, his developing selfhood is likely to be impaired. In response to a rejecting environment he can only make what use he can of his original endowment by calling upon those trends which are native to him. He can try to accommodate himself to his world by becoming compliant, or he can rebel against it by becoming aggressive, or he may move away from it by becoming detached. In other words, the original trends are not permitted to develop normally in expressive behavior but have to be used as defenses. Natural trends become distorted and take the form of an attempt to bend submissively, to assume mastery, or to remain unobtrusive.

The first of these responses, submissive bending, is prompted by the one fear in childhood which seems to override all others, namely, the fear of losing the love and support of the parents. Rather than risk this loss, the child will repress his native impulses and comply with his parents' wishes. Those objects and actions which are displeasing or inconvenient to them he will regard as taboo, things to be avoided at all costs. Strong guilt feelings will arise when the taboo is broken.

If the growing child can manage to free himself from this kind of parental tie, he will be able to develop his own sense of values and will feel guilty when he fails to realize them. "A feeling of 'functional guilt' is one which results from social suggestion, fear of taboos or of losing the love of others. A feeling of 'value guilt' is the genuine consciousness of having betrayed an authentic standard; it is a free judgment of the self by the self" (*Guilt and Grace* p. 64). If the child remains subject to the parental tie, he will not be free to do this. Instead, he will retain the old system of taboos and its accompanying system of guilt feelings.

In many people both structures remain side by side. These feelings of guilt are in part realistic in that they arise through failure to achieve self-chosen goals, and in part they are unrealistic in that they represent the survival of the infantile taboo system with its underlying fear of the loss of parental love. Such loss is always experienced as a form of punishment, and consequently all infantile guilt feelings are strongly tinged by the fear of punishment. Adult guilt feelings, on the other hand, are marked by a genuine sorrow for unachieved value, a feeling which is a spur toward the goals which have been missed.

3

The attitudes of others which do most to reinforce a person's exaggerated, infantile, false guilt feelings are those which are critical and judgmental toward his behavior. It is this fact that makes Tournier so critical of the rigid moralism often to be found in religious persons. "I recently met again a woman," he writes, "who had become burdened with feelings of inferiority and guilt by the stern upbringing of a domineering father. . . . While on holiday she had met a very dynamic minister and had told him about her difficulties. 'Have you been born again?' he asked her. She was again quite overcome with feelings of inferiority and guilt: 'It is true,' she mused, 'I have not been born again! But what must I do to achieve it? Others experience it and are freed, whereas it does not happen to me. My torment is proof of this' " (*Guilt and Grace* p. 23).

Religion, it is clear, can crush as well as liberate. Consider, for example, what must have been the reaction of a patient when her confessor, in an endeavor to prevent her marriage to a divorced man, remarked: "Do you not know that by marrying him you are bringing about his damnation and your own?" (*Guilt and Grace* p. 23).

Conversely, the attitudes which do most to encourage a person to unburden himself of his inner distress and to free him from his painful feelings of guilt are those of acceptance and understanding. "To whichever psychotherapeutic school we may give our allegiance, we know quite well that the essential condition for recovery is, on the doctor's side, a widely receptive attitude, free from all judgment. . . . The virtue of psychotherapy is the virtue of nonjudgment. We are overwhelmed by it and overjoyed, every time that we experience it afresh. We see in it a sign of God's grace" (*Guilt and Grace* p. 102).

In this respect the story of Jesus recorded in John 8, 3–11, in which he was asked to pronounce upon the behavior of an adulterous woman, was of particular significance to Tournier because it disclosed a remarkable embodiment of this particular attitude. "To the woman, taken in the act, convicted of sin, dumb with shame under accusations she cannot refute, Christ pronounces with divine authority, the word of absolution. He does not deny her guilt, He blots it out. . . . He does not suggest that she has not sinned, but He refuses to pronounce any condemnation" (*Guilt and Grace* pp. 111–112).

This is in line with a recent careful study of guilt. "*Guilt begins in love, is impossible without love, and paradoxically is only cured by love.*"[3] Tournier concurs with this view by stating succinctly that, without the relief that such an attitude brings, the guilty person is obliged to fall back on those defenses with which he has become equipped. He may find relief from the pain of guilt by *displacing* it on to a bodily ailment or accident, by *projecting* it on to others and blaming their faults rather than his own, (cf. *Guilt and Grace* pp. 138–139), by *self-justification* as instanced by the adulteress who "eats, and wipes her mouth, and says, 'I have done no wrong'" (Prov. 30.20), by the endeavor to drive it beyond conscious awareness (cf. *Guilt and Grace* p. 135), or by flight into moralism. This, Tournier believes, "stems from the sense of guilt which is so intolerable that men feel an overpowering need to preserve themselves from it. So there arises the question of paying lip-service to convention, of proving one's good conscience by conforming to the standards of one's environment, to some principles of a limited morality" (*Guilt and Grace* p. 127).

4

Repression of conscience, self-justification, projection, and the rest are, in the end, unsatisfactory ways of coping with guilt. The creative and fruitful way of handling it is by awareness, repentance, confession, and forgiveness. Unless this course is followed, the victims of guilt will find themselves in a vicious circle from which they cannot extract themselves. "Guilt—true or false . . . leads to anger, rebelliousness, and fear, and these in their turn lead on to evil. Evil consummated, in its turn, produces guilt" (*Guilt and Grace* p. 149).

The bonds of this circle are, in Tournier's view, only broken by a religion of grace which leads to repentance and thus to freedom from guilt (cf. *Guilt and Grace* p. 152). Such a liberating faith reaches our central and basic guilt which, to Tournier, arises from a sense of loss of divine guidance. "The whole of guilt is comprised in the fact of losing the guidance of God, shutting one's eyes to it, or refusing it. . . . Real life is life directed by God. Sin means to lose contact with God and to be guided by Him no longer" (*Guilt and Grace* pp. 171–172).

Tournier sees the severe passages of Scripture and in particular the messages of the prophets as aimed at provoking a sense of guilt in men who have forsaken God. "They were all raised up by God to denounce injustice and iniquity with the same severity, in order to awaken guilt in those who repressed it behind the smugness of men of piety" (*Guilt and Grace* p. 182). Yet the provocation was made with a view to deliverance. "The guilt that men are never able to efface, in spite of sacrifices, penance, remorse, and vain regrets, God Himself wipes away; and men are at once freed from their past and transformed" (*Guilt and Grace* p. 184).

To Tournier this freedom and transformation was mediated through Jesus Christ and particularly through his supreme act of self-sacrifice. "Salvation . . . is a person, Jesus Christ, who comes to us, comes to be with us, in our homes and in our hearts. Remorse is silenced by His absolution" (*Guilt and Grace* p. 187).

The royal way of entry into such freedom is by way of sincere confession. At least this is what Tournier himself found, and he never tires of pointing out to others the same requirement. Church membership and agreement with the Church's formularies and discipline did not prove to be sufficient for him. "I was a militant Church member; I truly believed not only in God and in Jesus Christ, but also in the Holy Spirit, the communion of saints, the forgiveness of sins, and the holy Catholic Church. But that, for me, was a belief rather than a living experience until the day when I met men who simply and honestly confessed their sins. . . . I threw myself wholeheartedly into the regular practice of confession . . ." (*Guilt and Grace* p. 202).

As a result of this experience Tournier found himself called to exercise a twofold ministry toward men and women burdened by a sense of guilt. For those caught in the toils of false guilt he uses psychological techniques; for those troubled by true guilt he acts as a kind of confessor, without usurping the confessional procedures that exist within the ecclesiastical structure. There is, he believes, an order of Melchizedek (Heb. 6.20; 7.1, 17, 21) in which they serve who fulfill a priestly function by being confessors and by mediating to others the promise of Divine forgiveness (cf. *Guilt and Grace* p. 210).

"General affirmations about the forgiveness of God have not at all the effect of a categorical, personal, individualized word pronounced with conviction on behalf of God and addressed to the man who has confessed his sin. . . . If, out of timidity, I evade this office, it is I who make myself guilty before God for eluding the mission He entrusts to me and the responsibility with which He has charged me in inducing this man to take me as a witness of his confession" (*Guilt and Grace* pp. 204–205).

8 ❖ Malaise and Rebirth

In *Escape from Loneliness* Tournier noted those factors in our society which are resistant to fellowship and thus open us more readily to the experience of loneliness. This is one aspect of the malaise of our time. He continued to examine other aspects of that malaise in a work entitled *The Whole Person in a Broken World*. The French title, *Désharmonie de la Vie Moderne,* is more precise in conveying the central idea of the book—the brokenness of man's life in our contemporary world.

It was natural for a psychiatric physician to think of the disharmony of modern life in terms of a neurosis. This kind of emotional disorder appears in a variety of forms; anxiety and phobic states, compulsions, conversion hysteria, and so on. Essentially, they occur largely as a result of internal conflict which reduces a person's functional efficiency, disrupts his personal relationships, and tends to make him overly self-preoccupied. The neurotic person exhibits patterns of behavior which are not only unsatisfactory to himself but also in the context of his living. In relation to himself and to others, his experience is one of *désharmonie*.

Tournier suggests that individual disharmony is a useful analogy for understanding the ills and pains of the modern world. If that is so, then, with a diagnosis at hand, it is easier to proceed to the task of healing.

When a therapist meets a neurotic patient and attempts to

help him, he begins (unless he is a behavior or reality therapist) to inquire about his earlier life with a view to discovering the origin and nature of the conflict from which he suffers. If he is an adolescent, the inquiry will cover his infancy, childhood, and school days. We use the example of an adolescent because Tournier thinks it meaningful to compare "this world with an anxiety-ridden adolescent who appears to be in conflict with his parents, his teachers, and society, but who is in reality in conflict with himself, that is, with his better self, — which is his repressed moral consciousness" (*Broken World* p. 68). The primitive history of mankind corresponds to the youth's infancy and childhood, the middle ages to his school years, and the post-renaissance period to the point at which he is now.

Like a disturbed adolescent the contemporary world suffers from a "neurosis of defiance" (*Broken World* p. 170). It is caught in the toils of rebellion but cannot come to terms with itself nor resolve its conflict. It exhibits the same anxiety, the same unproductiveness, and the same self-stultifying efforts at achieving its own salvation that a neurotic displays. "The efforts it makes to save itself bring it to ruin. The efforts it makes to arrest war pitch it into war . . ." (*Broken World* p. 9).

Modern man is suffering from massive repression. He "thinks — he has eliminated the world of values, the world of poetry, the world of moral consciousness; but he has only repressed it and is suffering from it . . ." (*Broken World* p. 11). Just as in the individual life neurosis manifests itself in anxiety, sterility, and self-defeating efforts at recovery, in the world at large there are manifest signs of its disorder and of attempts to put it right. Prevailing superstitions, like spiritualism and astrology, skeptical cynicism, and sectarian dogma (secular and religious) are symptoms of a more basic disorder. "The confusion of minds today is such that many men, in order to reassure themselves, cling with cramped fanaticism to some curious doctrine. . . . When a man is not sure of himself, he pretends to be the man who is unshakably convinced" (*Broken World* p. 34). This is due to the fact that modern man is repressing "the very principle of his inner harmony: the Spirit" (*Broken World* p. 35).

This kind of statement, of course, obliged Tournier to explain himself and to expound his understanding of spirit. What is man? What is the person? Where does spirit fit in? After some discussion of the matter, involving references to the works of Jean de Rougement and Arnold Stocker, Tournier offered his own interpretation and made use of the following diagram.

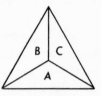

In the triangle the three bisectors delimit three small triangles which represent the body (A), the psyche (B), and the mind (C). The spirit is here represented only by a nonspatial "geometrical point," the point at which the bisectors intersect, the center. It is the center of the person, around which the whole man is ordered. It is invisible, it has no dimensions, and is not directly accessible. . . . It manifests itself outwardly and perceives exterior reality only through one of these three functions: its body, its imagination, or its thinking (*Broken World* pp. 53–54).

Here Tournier draws a distinction between the psyche, which expresses the imagination and affective aspects of human nature, and the mind, which indicates the intellectual and conceptualizing activities of man. It is the spirit, however, which is his central concept. It expresses itself through the body, the psyche, and the mind and at the same time assures their harmony and their unity. At least, it would do so if it occupied its true place in the hierarchy of the person. The psycho-mental aspect of man's nature has usurped the central, directive power of the spirit and has achieved an autonomy and a sovereignty of its own. "It is the imagination and the intellect, asserting their freedom from the normal healthy laws of life, that conceive the 'desire,' the thirst for hypertrophic, unlimited, insatiable gratification, sentimental or intellectual" (*Broken World* p. 56).

This is Tournier's interpretation of original sin. It is a condition of man's nature in which his craving for knowledge and gratification exceeds "those limits that are set by his physical and spiritual needs" (*Broken World* p. 56). It is a state of affairs in which the spirit is displaced from its hierarchical supremacy and repressed. The result is that "the vegetative functions, like the department heads in a factory, assume a relative autonomy [which brings about] disordered emotional reactions and functional disturbances" (*Broken World* p. 61).

Tournier concurs with the view of the spirit as the seat of "human feeling," of the "sense of justice," of the capacity to judge between good and ill (cf. *Broken World* p. 70). It is the home of conscience. To dethrone the spirit is thus to wound our sense of humanity and justice and to provoke an aggressive reaction as a result. "If we ignore the spirit in our conception of man, then society, the state, industry, and science likewise ignore the spiritual needs of man. They wound man and thus bring about that flood of aggressive reactions and conflicts which go on increasing in a vicious circle" (*Broken World* p. 71).

Since the spirit is the realm of values and commitment, its repression brings about an attachment to false values and thus to mistaken commitments. Two examples of this are seen in the importance attached to the myths of progress (cf. *Broken World* pp. 96–124) and of power (cf. *Broken World* pp. 125–143). These myths have exercised and still exercise considerable influence over most people in our time.

Meanwhile, the institutional churches, which are supposed

to bear the good news of the way in which we may be extricated from our difficulties, are remote from the situation where they are most needed. They have taken refuge in a domain of their own, remote from the political, social, economic, and cultural life of man. They need to demonstrate a new quality of life, formulate more clearly what the Gospel means in terms of the present situation, and proclaim that meaning with conviction and courage (cf. *Broken World* p. 160 f.). Tournier considers that there are hopeful signs pointing in this direction; in the end, however, he declares that the Church can be but an agent in bearing a message which basically can only have an individual application.

If our basic fault is the lost sovereignty of the spirit, then it needs to be restored to its rightful place by that which is beyond it—by the Holy Spirit. This is equated with the surrender of our whole being to the authority of Jesus Christ. "We must let God direct us in the use of our body and our goods, our work and our money, as well as in the realization of our feelings and our ideas. . . . This means that our devotion to Jesus Christ turns over to him not only our inner life but also our social life; that day by day we seek in quiet meditation a divine inspiration for the details of our activity" (*Broken World* p. 168).

2

Tournier, however, knew enough about human nature to realize that a proclamation of personal renewal by means of self-surrender was not sufficient. Was he not daily committed to the practice of a medicine of the person in which he made use of theoretical understandings of human nature and applied the technical skills associated with them. He employed theory and technique alike to bring about a shift in the balance of power within the lives of his patients.

What is the relation between technology (as used, for example, in psychotherapy) and faith? After he became committed to the medicine of the person, Tournier raised this question in a book entitled *The Person Reborn*. The French title of the work is a better guide to its purpose—*Technique et Foi*.

There are two ways of viewing human nature that must be held in synthesis. Faith sees man as a center of freedom and commitment, while some forms of personality theory see him as a balance of dynamic forces and structures. The imbalances within may have to be redressed before the commitment of faith becomes possible. Tournier does not hesitate to apply psychological techniques, but he sees them as preliminary to the commitment of faith. "Technology," he declares, "is not an end in itself. It ought only to prepare the way for a man to respond freely to the call of religious faith" *(Reborn* p. 7).

To break a person's complexes enables him to make a free response to his aspiration (cf. *Reborn* p. 35). And yet Tournier has to admit that the unveiling of repressed material by psychological techniques is itself a "spiritual" work. He says that the "always humbling process of bringing it [a repressed tendency] out into the light opens the door to a real experience of God's grace, even if no word of religion has been uttered by doctor or patient" *(Reborn* p. 36). On the other hand, continuing psychological analysis may result in being an end in itself and thus become a means of avoiding the basic issue of commitment. Certainly psychological technique cannot provide answers to the mystery of life's meaning. Faith is needed to complete the work of technology, while technology may often be a preliminary to the possibility of faith.

To this blend of technology and faith, Tournier applies a special term—soul healing *(Reborn* p. 38). He does not claim to be a psychiatrist in the exact sense, and where a patient manifests one of the severer forms of mental illness he does not hesitate to refer him to an appropriate authority for help. "I myself not being a psychiatrist, must avoid treating them without the assistance of a specialist colleague" *(Reborn* p. 227).

Healing calls for a deliberate emphasis on the ultimate commitments a person may make. It involves deep concern for others, patient listening, and the support of faith and prayer on the part of the healer. In other words, it relies heavily on what the healer himself is. "The ministry of soul healing does not finally depend on what we do for a person, but on what we are ourselves. The victory of faith must first be won in me. I must myself believe in God's grace for my patient, I must believe in his victory, in the dissolution of his problems, which are insoluble on the human level" (*Reborn* p. 38).

As practiced by a man of faith, soul healing means "taking a person into the presence of Christ" (*Reborn* p. 224). It is a means of opening him to the divine grace which brings an altogether new factor into the situation. "Grace, which touches man at the center of his being, introduces an entirely new element into the process, and gives it a new direction" (*Reborn* p. 123). Grace is more precious than medicine, advice, and psychological analysis, valuable and necessary as these things are (cf. *Reborn* p. 238).

3

Those who work on the borderland of faith and technology inevitably ask certain specific questions. It is an assumption of most psychologists, for example, that there is always a reason that people behave as they do; by "reason" is meant some causal situation occurring prior to the behavior in question. Thus psychological determinism presents itself for consideration. According to this viewpoint, we should regard the disturbed person as ill rather than wicked, diseased rather than malicious. Healing is called for, not moral judgment and correction.

Insofar as physical and psychological facts are concerned, Tournier accepted this deterministic stance but held that the person always remains free to make use of what he has. Thus there is a place for both determinism and responsibility (cf.

Reborn p. 116). At the same time the category of sinfulness remains, a category which suggests a fundamental flaw in human nature in virtue of which commitment to the divine will is withheld. Sin is not so much a condition as a disorder arising out of such a relationship.

So far as his attitude toward others was concerned, Tournier felt it wise to regard them as determined and himself as responsible. Examined from without, their behavior may be said to be marked by a total absence of responsibility. So far as Tournier is concerned, he prefers to regard himself as responsible (cf. *Reborn* p. 118). This makes for kindliness toward others and rigor toward oneself, which is desirable.

The relative merit of suggestion and faith was another problem with which Tournier was concerned. If the principle of suggestion—that ideas accepted by the mind even without grounds tend to actualize themselves and become facts—is a natural law, then can we not invoke the same principle to bring about behavioral change and healing? Is not so-called faith but a form of suggestion?

Tournier holds that the question hides a confusion. Suggestion is a process that undoubtedly enters into the formation of emotional disorders. The attitudes and example of others, their accepted standards and expectations convey to us the notion that some forms of behavior are wrong. "Suggestion," Tournier writes, "is the fundamental cause of most sexual disorders, such as impotence [and] frigidity . . ." (*Reborn* p. 155).

But there is more to the cure of functional disorders than the giving of counter-suggestion. Their formation may be due to suggestion, but they are maintained by factors of unconscious origin. Insomnia, for example, may be brought about by worry or by illness, but it only remains as a continuing ailment if other factors beyond conscious awareness are operative. It may, for example, express "a protest against the waste of time spent in sleeping" (*Reborn* p. 148) or indicate a badly regulated life, say "one that is too intellectual for a practical temperament" (*Reborn* p. 149). Agoraphobia, too, may express a desire for independence which was repressed in childhood by domineering and possessive parents. To suggest to the sufferer that he will feel more confident when he enters open spaces may help, but it will not be nearly as effective as the patient disentangling of his complexes by analytical psychology.

In religious faith, too, suggestion is at work, but faith itself goes beyond suggestion. It presupposes a personal relationship between God and the believer "which develops as love and which, through love, shapes itself in life as that free, voluntary trust which is what we ordinarily mean by faith."[1]

It includes belief, commitment and obedience to God. Yet it is not always sure, bold and strong; it is sometimes hesitant and weak. "Faith," notes Tournier, "retains its humility and trepidation, it is nevertheless the source of the only enlightenment that never disappoints" (*Reborn* p. 175).

4

It was natural for Tournier to pass from the notion of faith and the related idea of rebirth to one of his central themes, that of meditation. It is interesting to note the thoughts of another author, Dr. R. S. Lee, who has written from a Freudian perspective. "The constructive value of meditation lies in the way it deepens the channel from the id to the ego, from the unconscious to the conscious, from desire to attainment This depends more on the imagination than on the will. . . . It gives wisdom and understanding, and it also gives inner unity and freedom. It is creative in its effect. . . . The material deliberately chosen as the subject of meditation is fed into the mind and there absorbed to become part of the personality. Call it waiting upon God, if you like. It is certainly the contemplation of the divine and it gives the divine element the opportunity to come to life in us."[2]

Tournier's meditation is a daily exercise of at least an hour

during which he reflects on biblical passages and other spiritual
classics, engages in self-examination, and seeks guidance for
the day ahead. He also uses the time to pursue "some intellectual task under [God's] guidance" (*Reborn* p. 178). It provides an occasion for becoming entirely open to God. "If we
bring our minds back again and again to God, we shall by the
same inevitable law be gradually giving the central place to
God, not only in our inner selves, but also in our practical
everyday lives" (*Reborn* p. 179).

Although guidance is frequently sought in meditation, it is
by no means the only fruit of Tournier's quiet hour. It is a
means of review and correction as well as of obtaining direction
for the way ahead. It cultivates "the ability to perceive clearly
both our faults and our vocation" (*Healing* p. 265). For example, one of the earliest experiences Buchman had was to
see the mistakes in his own behavior and to apologize for
them.

It is, moreover, a therapeutic measure of the greatest importance to the person undertaking it. To look honestly and
carefully within during such moments is to become aware of
factors within the self that need to be integrated into the total
person. "It leads him into the integration of contradictory
tendencies which hitherto were tearing him apart" (*Resist or
Surrender* p. 63). Profound changes occur within the person
which forward his own personal growth. Tournier likens the
results of such meditation to those of analysis. "Meditation . . .
enlarges the field of consciousness and reveals the hidden un-
dercurrents of the mind in a way that is very similar to the
operation of psychoanalysis . . ." (*Reborn* p. 12).

Perhaps the ripest fruit of meditation is to foster and deepen
the quality of faith. The daily habit of placing oneself resolutely before God activates a deep sense of reliance on God in
virtue of which life can be lived courageously, joyously, creatively, and in gratitude. Faith breeds not only the sense of
adventure in living but achieves such a radical transformation

of the attitudes, values, and purposes of the self in which it is present that the person can properly be described as reborn.

As a physician, Tournier was quick to discern the fruits of faith in the body itself. He understood illness to have a voice of its own whereby it declares in the body some important truth about the person of the sufferer. He cites, for example, the condition of phlebitis (inflammation of the veins) which calls for the ordinary diagnostic and treatment skills of the physician. But it may also indicate something about the patient. "Repeated attacks of phlebitis in the legs," Tournier declares, "may symbolize a fear of moving forward in life" (*Casebook* p. 182). The sufferer may fear to assume responsibility or take initiative. In addition to the skill of the physician, this patient will need the confidence born of faith if he is to move forward with courage and hope. With the dawning of faith he can be said to be reborn as a total person, and that renewal may declare itself in his body as much as in any other area of his life. "When he turns back to God, man . . . becomes creative once more, instead of destructive" (*Reborn* p. 235).

There may be factors in the total situation of the patient, however, which mean that his physical condition cannot be cured by the skills known to medical science. In these circumstances faith may have to exercise itself, not in bodily healing, but in the courageous bearing of a condition which cannot be cured.

9 ❖ Person and Vocation

The change of focus in Tournier's professional career from scientific medicine to the medicine of the person also explains the importance he began to attach to the idea of vocation. As a Christian he saw the world as part of a coherent plan laid down by a beneficent Creator who engages in his work of creation and in his endeavor to overcome evil and restore the lives of men. He summons man to share this endeavor with him, each according to his particular ability. The God who speaks can address his call to everyone who will listen. The capacity for obedient response lies in every man in that he is free to "choose what attitude to adopt toward God, life, events, and other people, and finally discern his vocation" (*Adventure* p. 220).

To Tournier vocation means that each man must live and work so as to respond to the divine claim made upon him. Having once committed himself in this direction, he must reflect upon the details of his day-to-day response by remaining open and obedient to God, particularly in his times of meditation. "Meditation is an open attitude—open in two directions: toward God and toward material life. It is a trusting and attentive attitude of waiting" (*Adventure* p. 215).

Thus called and open to God's continuing guidance, Tournier found himself fulfilling his ministry in a given place. His service was located somewhere. "The important thing for every man is not only to find a place, but to find his own true

place, the one God wills for him" (*Place* p. 168). Only in this
way can a man participate fully in the divine adventure and
be encouraged to do his work in a creative and adventurous
spirit. Indeed, location and the spirit of adventure could be
described as two of the most important aspects of vocation and
are the main topics of two of his books, *A Place for You* and
The Adventure of Living.

2

It is obvious that to exist as humans we have to occupy a
place, an area of living space. It then becomes natural for us
to invest our energies in our place, to become attached to it,
and to grow fond of it. This scene supports and gives stability
to our living, as do the human relations we enpoy in it. When
we are obliged to uproot ourselves and to move elsewhere, the
sense of loss begins to obtrude. We feel a pang of regret, experience a degree of sorrow, and though we set out with high
hopes, find them tinged with regret. We are losing our place.

There are extensions to this idea of place to which Tournier
wished to draw attention. Our bodies, for example, form part
of our place; indeed, it is only by means of the body that we
can sense and experience the place which surrounds. Happy
the man who is comfortable with this particular aspect of his
place. "Accepting life means accepting that one has a body and
identifying oneself with it, as well as accepting the limitations
it imposes on our ambitions, especially when it is ill, infirm, or
old" (*Place* p. 66). Unless a man can accept his physique, sex,
age, and state of health, he cannot be at home in his place.
When he becomes ill, illness will be a part of his place which
he will be wise to accept. "Sickness is a new place which he
must of necessity accept . . ." (*Place* p. 70). He will have more
energy available for the process of recovery if he does not allow
himself to be overcome by fruitless regret and bitter complaint that he is not what he once was.

Our own personality is another aspect of our place with which it is important to be at one. Our genetic stock and all we have been and are now is something given, a place on which we have to build our present relationships, endeavors, and aspirations for the future. Tournier felt that this notion was of particular importance to Christians since part of their calling consists of abandoning themselves in self-surrender and self-sacrifice. One of the New Testament passages which speaks of this is clear enough: "Anyone who wishes to be a follower of mine must leave self behind; he must take up his cross, and come with me. Whoever cares for his own safety is lost; but if a man will let himself be lost for my sake and for the Gospel, that man is safe" (Mark 8:34–35, NEB). Tournier met many patients who, though anxious to obey such a direction, had little sense of being at home with themselves. The remedy was obvious to Tournier. "Self-assertion must come before self-denial" (*Place* p. 115). "We must first exist, defend ourselves, succeed, assert ourselves, before showing ourselves generous" (*Place* p. 111). "One must have a place before one can give it up. One must receive before giving, exist before abandoning oneself in faith" (*Place* p. 136). It was this consideration which enabled Tournier to see that therapeutic measures may sometimes have to be preliminary to making the response of faith.

It is easy to understand that a man may become so attached to his place that he becomes either unwilling or unable to give it up. This will apply particularly to those who, being in part emotionally damaged and lacking an inner sense of competence in living, seek security outside of themselves, either by clinging to people or to places. For example, the overly dependent wife, who cannot allow her husband out of her sight, or the housebound person are not free to leave their place. The free man, on the other hand, can give up his place and move on. "Every man must come some day to the turning point in his destiny when he must let go of what he has received, on pain of remaining its prisoner and becoming lost in it" (*Place* p. 145).

To all of us some places become so supporting, so protective, so safe, that it is hard to let them go; to some, it is particularly difficult. A sick person, for example, who has been the object of skillful nursing care and the recipient of widespread solicitude may find it hard to get better, for this will involve the abandonment of a place of comfort for one less secure. "To get well is to lose the protection, care, and support which one received as a sick person. To get well is once more to face responsibilities, risks, and disappointments from which one has been excused by illness . . ." (*Place* p. 147).

In the moments of transition from one place to another we find ourselves in a zone of uncertainty and thus lack the support of the previous place. "There is a place that must be left before we can find a new place, and in between there is a place without a place, a place without support, a place which is not a place, since a true place is a support" (*Place* p. 160). The great transitions in our human pilgrimage—from childhood to youth, from adolescence to adulthood, from membership in the family to independence, from marriage to widowhood, from maturity to age, from life to death—are fraught with anxiety. Therapeutic interference also increases anxiety before it relieves it because the subject is engaged in moving from one emotional stance (or place) to another. His inner readjustment and change of attitude is a movement from an uncomfortable place to another in which he can be happier and more fully human. This kind of movement toward personal maturity and greater achievement cannot occur without developing the quality of openness to the future. We must become better able to sustain the spirit of adventure.

3

Merely to be located in one's place is not enough. We are the bearers of an innate thrust toward growth, achievement, and fulfillment, and this has to be accepted as part of our make-up in the same way as our need for stability in a place. Man has a need for personal adventure which is peculiar to him. "This whole, enormous, costly, and constant effort to make some small mark on the great chess board of life has its source in man's very human instinct of creative adventure" (*Adventure* p. 100). Personal living is an adventure to which we are obliged to commit ourselves in faith and conviction and with a readiness to accept the risks involved.

This general principle has a particular application so far as vocation is concerned. To embrace a goal which love suggests, to commit oneself to it, and to sustain that commitment continuously and creatively is not only to fulfill oneself as a man but, in a very real sense, to experience our likeness to the Divine Adventurer. "Man, therefore, as it were feels his divinity when he commits himself totally in an adventure. . . . He experiences in some measure his resemblance to God" (*Adventure* p. 71).

This point of view is bound up with Tournier's understanding of the religious life as the guided life. "Religion means binding ourselves to God, abandoning ourselves to him, asking him to guide us. . . . Sincerely to seek God's guidance remains the surest method of living the adventure of our lives. . . ." (*Adventure* pp. 188, 187).

Not all religion, unfortunately, encourages such an adventurous attitude. Religion can be a means of safety for somebody who is insecure; its standardized and routine procedures may be sought as a means of support by the dependent person. A living faith is something different. Tournier's experience made him aware of this, and he does not tire of underlining its truth and reminding his readers of the moment when its truth dawned on him. "All converts have changed from a routine of religion to an adventure of religion. I myself have a keen sense of this kinship of the spirit. . . . When my wife and I came into contact with the Oxford Group Movement [we] . . . were thereby shown how abstract and theo-

retical, how little incarnate in our real life, our faith was . . ."
(*Adventure* pp. 25–26).

Tournier's commitment to the medicine of the person was
a remarkable adventure and two elements within it reveal the
extent of his commitment to adventure: his writing and his
therapeutic method. That Tournier's attempt to become an
author was fraught with risk and difficulty may be judged from
the fact that he submitted his first manuscript to six people
before approaching a publisher, only to find that none of these
friends encouraged him to proceed to publication (cf. *Adventure* p. 48). He persisted in the undertaking, however, but discovered that several publishers rejected his work before one
agreed to undertake it. Even now a new book is still an adventure for him. "I am an amateur in my workshop," he writes,
"and derive the keenest joy from working there in wood and
metal. But I am also an amateur psychotherapist, amateur
philosopher, amateur theologian, amateur lecturer, and amateur writer. For me, to write a book is not to teach or to
create a work of literature; it is to have an adventure in company with my readers both known and unknown" (*Adventure*
p. 42).

If there is novelty and risk in undertaking any adventure,
Tournier certainly showed that he was prepared for it by
adopting a distinctive therapeutic method. His therapeutic
intervention rests heavily, as it does for any therapist, on the
quality of the relationship that he can establish with his
patients. Tournier felt, however, that his work could only be
effective if he was prepared to commit himself to patients in
the same way that he invited patients to commit themselves
to him. His association with the Oxford Group had taught
him the value of "sharing"; he now applied that lesson, with
obvious therapeutic intent, to his work as a doctor. Therapy
became an adventure in self-commitment. "I think what dis-
tinguishes me most clearly from the specialists in psychotherapy
of all the varying schools is this commitment of my person in

the dialogue with the patient, my readiness to talk to him about my own problems" (*Adventure* p. 68). Naturally this is only done when it is likely to prove beneficial to the patient and certainly not at the outset of treatment. Tournier recognizes that the patient "would be put off right at the start if, in order to make him feel that we are nearer to each other than he thinks, I talked to him about my own weakness" (*Place* p. 188).

This remark not only suggests the importance of timing in therapeutic work but indicates that the same principle applies to vocation as a whole. God not only wants a man working adventurously in a particular place, but he needs him there at a particular time. A man must not only seek his place but bide his time, just as a good doctor, having a biological view of the soul's growth, knows that each event has its time and is therefore content to wait for it (cf. *Escape* p. 49).

4

Tournier considered the principle of vocation to apply as much to marriage as to work and achievement. Tournier frequently refers to sex, marriage, and the family not only because these are important topics in themselves but also because he frequently met sexual and marital difficulties in the patients he encountered. He deplored the false shame and the deep sense of guilt associated with sex in the minds of so many. Heavy guilt feelings over masturbation, for example, were frequent. He felt these were exaggerated by the childrearing practices common in the society in which his patients were nurtured, but he also thought that true guilt is attached to the act. He speaks in one place of an inner voice accusing us of violating an order of nature, for seeking solitary pleasure instead of a shared pleasure which generates community (cf. *Strong and Weak* p. 80). Such guilt feelings disappear when sex is brought into the service of love and when it is enjoyed in the context of marriage. Here, however much it may be devalued, deified, or despised elsewhere, sex is at home and assists the fulfillment of human nature (cf. *Casebook* p. 67).

If to love is to understand, know, care for, and serve another's good, then marriage is the best context in which it may be expressed, cultivated, and deepened. There are natural differences, other than physiological ones, between men and women which makes them complement each other in life generally but particularly in marriage where there is an enduring self-commitment (cf. *Seasons* pp. 36–37). Marriage is a relationship which can only be fully enjoyed by those who are free to give themselves. "Men need to give because they need to give themselves, and all their gifts are signs of that deep-seated and universal desire to give oneself. To live is to commit oneself" (*Gifts* p. 56). For men and women truly to complement one another in marriage there has to be understanding and openness between them. Tournier has expounded this principle with deep sympathy in a little work entitled *To Understand Each Other*. He writes that to express oneself openly requires courage to overcome the fear of being judged or the fear of receiving advice. To encourage openness in one's partner, one must be ready to listen attentively and to receive in a warm and kindly way what is expressed. "In order really to understand, we need to listen, not to reply. We need to listen long and attentively. In order to help another to open his heart, we have to give him time, asking only a few questions, as carefully as possible, in order to help him better to explain his experience" (*To Understand* p. 25). He adds that self-expression occurs only if a person can feel deeply loved.

By means of their openness toward each other, the partners to a marriage are drawn closely together. But there is also a place for apartness and for differences of opinion. "Couples who become identified to the point of not being able to leave each other's side and of never having a difference of opinion are less unified than they believe" (*Secrets* p. 55). There is a place for conflict in marriage particularly since women have achieved a greater degree of independence than ever before. In the process of its resolution conflict can be creative. It is helpful, however, if both partners can acknowledge their own contribution to the resolution (cf. *Guilt and Grace* pp. 137–138).

On the other hand, conflict can become so deep and so acute that the partners may develop patterns of behavior which become destructive toward each other and their children. Divorce may be the solution but, in Tournier's view, only if the partners had never discovered the meaning of living according to God's guidance. "I know that there is always a solution other than divorce to a marital conflict, if we are really prepared to seek it under God's guidance" (*Reborn* p. 71).

Tournier is plainly influenced by the experience of his own marital life. He and his wife have tried to make their relationship as transparent as possible. "Transparency," he writes, "is the law of marriage and the couple must strive for it untiringly at the cost of confession which is always new and sometimes very hard" (*Secrets* p. 50). They have been assisted in this endeavor by the practice of joint meditation which has not only brought them guidance for their way but a disclosure to each other of their most intimate thoughts and feelings (cf. *Secrets* p. 57). They have come to know, at least in part, the meaning of what Tournier calls "total marriage." "There is only one kind of marriage that is really creative: total marriage. In it there is achieved bodily communion, emotional communion, spiritual communion, and if I may so express it, a communion between the three kinds of communion" (*Escape* p. 182).

As a means of human fulfillment, marriage is an aspect of vocation. In *The Seasons of Life* Tournier sees the life cycle as a series of unfolding seasons, spring giving way to summer and summer to autumn and so on. If spring is the time of childhood, youth and early adulthood, summer is the time for career, marriage and home-making. There is a law of summer

which says that for most people marriage is part of their way
of life. But what of the single man or woman? If celibacy is
consciously chosen as a person's way of life, it can be accepted
as part of his own self-fulfillment. This is God's way for that
person, and it can be embraced gladly and creatively if he has
come to terms with the meaning of his sexuality and parental
impulses and can offer these as part of his vocation.

For others, the celibate way may not be self-chosen. This
way of life may present peculiar difficulties and special chal-
lenges. Tournier writes sympathetically of the celibate woman.
"It is not only a matter of being deprived of the sex life. It is
not only a matter of being deprived of motherhood, which is a
much more painful deprivation for many women. It is a matter
of the loneliness which is so contrary to the needs of a woman,
having to live both sorrows and joys alone, unable to share
them with a husband who makes them his own" (*Adventure*
p. 132).

But, as between love in marriage and love in service, there
is no priority in value. The single person may meet the challenge of celibacy and fulfill his vocation creatively. "The self-
giving woman, resolutely throwing herself into an inspired
and outgoing vocation with the impulse of love that her heart
needs to express, has found her home and spiritual family in
the sick, the lonely, the poor, and the children whom she has
met on her way" (*Escape* p. 85).

10 ❖ Comment and Response

Perhaps a brief review of the way we have come may provide the best preface to a general estimate of Tournier's thought and work.

Some of the more significant factors of Tournier's formation as a person and as a doctor occupied us at the outset. We noted that, as a result of a remarkable spiritual experience, he decisively reappraised his work and undertook the practice of what he calls the medicine of the person. This was a healing ministry to the total person of the patient in the course of which Tournier was able to draw upon his knowledge and experience of medical science, his acquaintance with modern schools of psychotherapy, and his religious insights and commitment. This task naturally raised some basic questions in his mind and obliged him to articulate his understanding of the meaning of persons, a consideration of some of the more profound experiences which are common to us all. Thus Tournier was led to inquire into the nature of fear, guilt, and loneliness.

"It has been said of medicine," he wrote, "that its duty is sometimes to heal, often to afford relief, and always to bring consolation" (*Casebook* p. 220). Although this has been his purpose throughout his medical career, his concern has been with the total person; he has aimed not only at giving relief from troublesome symptoms but also at bringing about personality change and at assisting in the process of growth towards personal fulfillment. We have tried to outline this meaning in the discussion of rebirth and vocation.

It has been tempting to criticize particular ideas and to query various statements and interpretations, but to have done so earlier would not only have prolonged our discussion but may have blurred the outline of what was being presented. Withholding criticism, however, should not be understood as implying agreement with everything expounded. Since we are concerned with the broad sweep of Tournier's thought and work we can leave aside critical details. It is much more important to attempt a fair estimate of the whole.

2

We may begin to comment on his professional work with a reference to a piece of interesting and highly instructive research carried out at the Tavistock Clinic, London, some years ago by Dr. Michael Balint.[1] Balint, his wife and colleague Enid Balint, and a group of fourteen general practitioners met for half a day per week over a period of more than two years to discuss the doctor-patient relationship and the dynamic interaction which occurs when a patient brings a complaint to his doctor's attention. A number of important conclusions emerged from these discussions. It became clear that a patient's condition could be diagnosed at different levels.

Some forms of illness, particularly those which are apparently caused by some external agent such as a wounding object, a chemical, or a germ, are easily diagnosed. Other forms are not nearly so well-defined. They seem to grow from within the patient as if they were a physical expression of conflicts deep within him.

The shape of the illness, too, seems to be significant because it sometimes reflects in its outline the character pattern of the patient. It has its own voice and can declare its meaning to those who are attuned to hear.

The Tavistock inquiry not only revealed varying levels of illness and their relation to the general personality pattern of the patient, but also noted subjective elements introduced into diagnosis and treatment by the doctor himself. However much he may try to preserve an objective and scientific stance, the physician cannot exclude his own personality from the process. At some stage or other, for example, he is likely to contribute assurance and advice. He often shows that he has a vague yet firm idea about how a patient ought to behave when ill. He exhibits a tendency to convert the patient to his way of thinking. Balint has called this the doctor's apostolic mission or function.[2] Moreover, the doctor cannot avoid bringing to his patient his own characteristics as a person. One physician will be a benign authoritarian; another will be eager to be considered a good doctor; a third will show unwearying patience and acceptance, and so on.

These observations draw attention to the obvious psychological aspects of general practice. When a physician becomes aware of these aspects and is prepared to diagnose illness at its deeper levels and help his patients with their problems in living, he is introducing a psychotherapeutic element.

Tournier, too, has recognized that relief from physical symptoms often depends on readjusting the emotional life of the patient and on bringing about some degree of personality change. He chose to call his work the medicine of the person, partly as a reminder that he was concerned with the person as a whole, and partly as a way of suggesting that there were distinctive features which he brought to its practice.

Of these features, Tournier's emphasis on the importance of the religious dimension of life has opened him to a good deal of criticism from psychiatrists, particularly those in the western world. Interestingly enough, he has met with a good deal of sympathy from Islamic psychiatrists with whom he has held discussions in Teheran and elsewhere.

A psychiatrist might object that Tournier's emphasis on re-

ligious factors introduces into the therapeutic setting an element which detracts from its objectivity and scientific stance.
To this it seems fair to reply that the therapeutic setting cannot be totally objective. Balint's work has shown the presence
of an apostolic mission in the work of a general practitioner;
such a function is present in an even greater degree in the work
of a psychiatrist. The difference between Tournier and his
critics is that they see their apostolic function differently.
Tournier cannot help seeing it in the light of his own religious
experience with its own distinctively Christian focus. To him
"the true God is never simply beyond but also within people.
. . . God is present in man's becoming man. God is graciously
present in the human growth that makes man a free subject
open to faith, hope, and love."[3]

Despite the importance Tournier attaches to the *patient's
orientation toward God* and to the means of deepening and
enhancing that orientation, no one could be more outspoken
than he against the dangers of mistaken piety and rigid moralism. "I cannot keep count," he writes, "of the number of people
in whom religion, the love of God, and the desire to serve
him . . . lead only to a life of sterility, sadness, and anxiety"
(*Reborn* p. 82). Tournier would free religion from neurotic and
destructive elements and open the way to a final commitment
which is free and fulfilling. Without such a commitment no
one can be considered to be on the path to wholeness, or rather,
to those preliminary and partial aspects of it which alone are
possible to finite creatures in a temporal world.

Another distinctive feature of Tournier's medicine of the person is his *therapeutic method.* In current psychiatric and therapeutic practice the relationship of doctor and patient plays a
crucial role. Its nature has been defined by Herbert Fingarette
as accepting and compassionate, yet detached and uninvolved.
In respect to his patient, the helper "participates in the agony
and in the contest of the spirit, helps him to bring victory out
of defeat, a new birth out of death. Yet, enlightened, he is
somehow above the contest, an unaffected helper."[4]

Tournier would entirely agree with this definition of dis-interested love and understanding. Yet, unlike others, he has never felt inconsistent with this stance when he speaks about himself in a way which is both frank and humble. In his prac-tice there is a tendency to share himself and his experiences with his patients.

A third distinctive feature in Tournier's medicine of the person is *the means he uses to maintain and enhance his own self-awareness.* In the study mentioned earlier Balint ob-served that *"the acquisition of therapeutic skill does not con-sist only of learning something new; it inevitably also entails a limited, though considerable, change in the doctor's person-ality."*[5] Such change must be maintained and deepened. For some psychotherapists this will indicate a brief return to their own analysis; for others it will involve participation in a group of colleagues. Tournier has filled this need by his association with the Bossey Group and by meditation. He observes the daily practice of placing himself resolutely before God, of becoming open to God and thus allowing his doubt, guilt, and fear to come to the surface. It is a review of feeling in the presence of the transcendent. "I try," he says, "to maintain the mind of a child."[6]

It seems fair to say, then, that the medicine of the person in-cludes all the features of psychotherapy and distinctive features of its own.

3

We turn now to consider Tournier as thinker, interpreter of the human situation, and writer. In reading Tournier's books I have been impressed by the *anecdotal method* which he favors, by *the evangelistic and hortatory style* to which he resorts, and by a noticeable *individualism* with respect to his theory of social change.

In one place Tournier remarks that his thoughts "are born of the experiences I have with my patients, and of all they tell me about their lives" (*Place* p. 171). It is natural for a man of such wide sympathy and compassion to focus his attention on the meaning of events and experiences in the lives of others. "My life's work," he declares in *The Adventure of Living*, "has taught me that living experiences attract and help people more than theories" (p. 53).

As physician, therapist, and spiritual confidant of so many, Tournier has been able to build an enormous store of anecdote which illustrate his principles and drive home his points. Such anecdotes have the attraction and insistent appeal of a drama which engages and involves an audience while it entertains them. I am sure that this anecdotal element in Tournier's writing is one of the chief reasons for his popularity and helpfulness. It is also in line with the general approach he makes to his work. He entered medicine not so much as a means of undertaking scientific research but as a means of helping people. His focus has been on the personal and on the concrete, on the way people respond to this situation and that. Theoretical formulation does not suit him whereas the anecdotal style does.

There are weaknesses, however, as well as strength in this method. It is easy, for example, to cite a number of experiences which differ in contextual detail but illustrate the same principle. This style may give the impression that the author is repeating himself. The element of repetition, however, is more apparent for another reason. A strong evangelistic and hortatory note is heard in all that he writes. He has a gospel to declare (for which he is to be commended), but the frequent reference to it is usually accompanied by a call to personal surrender and obedience to the will of God and by an appeal to the advantages of living under guidance. The guided person lives more simply and with far less strain. He hands over his life to God. He renounces grand personal plans. He lives each moment as it comes. Almost without exception, his larger works outline, often in sincere and moving language,

the meaning and importance of meditation. I do not wish to
discount the usefulness of what is said. I merely draw attention
to the fact that it is said repeatedly. Yet, reinforcement is a
necessary element in learning, so this repetition may have a
wisdom and a force of its own.

As I see it, Tournier's greatest limitation lies in the basically
individualistic approach he takes to the problem of social
change. Here, I think, he has allowed himself to accept too
uncritically the tradition of the Oxford Group which in other
respects was so helpful to him. I am not saying that Tournier's
work lacks social concern, for his personal career contradicts
such a suggestion.

"Christ's method of changing the world," he writes, "is to
use the spirit that radiates from a person who has experienced
a change of heart" (*Reborn* p. 213). Social change, then, can
only be expected to come from transformed members of society who are healing units within it. To become a healing
unit the individual will need to confront his own failures
honestly and to undergo amendment of life. "Instead of de-
nouncing and attacking all the shortcomings of society, [Christ]
calls us to recognize our own shortcomings, so that we may
become a healthy unit in society" (*Reborn* p. 213).

This is a plain declaration of the social strategy of the Oxford Group. John C. Bennett drew attention to this some years
ago. "Their method is to seek out strategic individuals in
order to convert them, to bring them into a complete reorientation of personal life so that their wills are surrendered to God.
These converts . . . live 'guided' lives, receiving their guidance
directly from God in moments of illumination which are cultivated as part of a daily discipline. When men are so con-
verted it is expected that they will inevitably deal effectively
with the social evils in which their lives are involved."[7]

As Bennett points out, this assumes that dedicated people
can be sufficiently free from the rationalizations whereby even
godly people defend their position of power and privilege, and

that such people have adequate wisdom to deal with social evil. It also overlooks the multiple causes of social ills and the fact that such ills, be they exploitation, inequality of opportunity, racial discrimination, war, poverty, or pollution, have their roots outside the deliberate choices of individual men. Without change in political and economic structures, and in the laws which govern them, even the most enlightened and humane of men are powerless to give substance to their ideals. Social evil has to be remedied both by enlightened individuals and by political and economic measures organized on a large scale with mass community support. It will be possible to combat water pollution, for example, only by a concentrated and combined effort on the part of scientists, industry, lawmakers, and the public. The sources of pollution will have to be identified, public attitudes towards the problem will have to be changed by a long process of reeducation, and laws will have to be passed to prevent, say, the dumping of untreated sewage into our rivers.

4

Individualism as a theory of social change is, however, to be distinguished from individualism as a central emphasis. No one could charge Tournier with the latter since he is so sensitive to the meaning and value of community. His own personal pilgrimage, his experience in the Oxford Group, and his work with the Bossey Group are sufficient proof of this. So, too, is his family and community life in Troinex.

His attitude toward the Church as an institution, despite his criticism of it, is likewise determined by an appreciation of its value as a community of believers. It is a source of continuing regret to him that the potential of this community is so often unrealized. Men everywhere exhibit signs of deep religious need, yet institutional religion seems unable to meet that need. It almost appears to remain aloof from it. Coun-

selors, therapists, physicians, and psychiatrists deal day by day
with the issues of life's meaning and with the problem of guilt
(both of which are religious concerns), while the Church seems
to be preoccupied with other, more trivial, and less relevant
concerns. Yet Tournier himself owes much to institutional religion and still acknowledges the important place it must play
in men's lives.

No estimate of Tournier's work, however, could be valid
without stressing again his qualities of compassion and faith.
He is not given to abstract formulation. He has been content
to remain theoretically eclectic and to learn from Freud, Jung,
Adler and, their successors. His concern has been to apply this
knowledge to meet the needs of persons. His compassion for
them is born of a sense of their dignity, worth, and possibilities,
especially when they can allow themselves to be grasped by an
ultimate concern. Their blindness, stupidity, and pride emerge
in anecdotes throughout his books, but in the healing relationship one begins to discern the dawning of freedom and creativity, of aspiration and hope. In a period when we are caught
in a vast process of dehumanization and when the fear and
hatred of being human is so widespread, this emphasis is both
timely and helpful.

Tournier's faith in the human possibility is rooted in his
faith in God. It is God who can transform and guide men's
lives, and it is God who uses the healing process to further
these ends. If faith is a radical trust in God as all-sufficient, then
Tournier has been content to live and work as a man of faith,
or, if you prefer, as a man of God.

Notes

Chapter 1   *A Doctor's Formation*

1. A poem by Louis Tournier, *Les Voix de la Cathédrale,* was published in Geneva in 1867. Other poems appeared in a short commemorative essay by Louis Choisy entitled *Louis Tournier* and published in 1899.
2. A copy of this letter is in the writer's possession.

Chapter 2   *Decisive Encounter*

1. The following account relies on a number of sources but is particularly indebted to Walter Houston Clark, *The Oxford Group: Its History and Significance* (New York: Bookman Associates, 1951).
2. A. J. Russell, *For Sinners Only* (London: Hodder & Stoughton, 1932), p. 58.
3. Peter Howard, *Frank Buchman's Secret* (London: Heineman, 1961), p. 21.
4. See Philip Jacob Spener, *Pia Desideria* trans. Theodore G. Tappert (Philadelphia: Fortress Press, 1964).
5. Kenneth Scott Latourette, *A History of Christianity* (New York: Harper & Row, 1953), p. 895.
6. H. Hensley Henson, *The Oxford Group* (London: Oxford University Press, 1933), p. 4.
7. A. J. Russell, *op. cit.,* pp. 42–43.
8. *Ibid.,* p. 319.
9. W. H. Clark, *op. cit.,* p. 28.
10. *Ibid.,* pp. 255–256.
11. From an address entitled "A Dialogue between Doctor and Patient" before the Third International Congress of Christian

Physicians at Oslo, 16–20 July, 1969, and published in J. B. Natvig and N. J. Lavik (eds.), *The Responsibility of the Christian Physician in the Modern World* (Oslo: Universitetsforlaget, 1969).

12. Peter Howard, *op. cit.*, p. 119.

Chapter 3   *The Medicine of the Person*

1. "I have not the mind of a professor," he once candidly admitted in personal conversation.
2. Leslie D. Weatherhead, *Psychology, Religion and Healing* (London: Hodder & Stoughton, 1952), p. 315. Italics his.
3. Eric Wittkower, *A Psychiatrist Looks at Tuberculosis* (London: The National Association for the Prevention of Tuberculosis, 1949), pp. 139–140.
4. Karl A. Menninger, *The Human Mind* (New York: Knopf, 1964), p. 23.
5. See E. Kretschmer, *Physique and Character* trans. W. J. H. Sprott (London: Routledge, Kegan Paul, 1951), pp. 20–37, 67–85. Tournier cites Kretschmer and other authors in developing this theme in *The Strong and the Weak*.
6. T. W. Adorno *et al.* (eds.), *The Authoritarian Personality* (New York: Harper & Row, 1950), p. 747.

Chapter 4   *Loneliness*

1. See Aniela Jaffé, *C. G. Jung: Memories, Dreams, Reflections,* trans. R. & C. Winston (London: Collins, 1967), p. 58.
2. *Ibid.,* pp. 388–389.
3. See P. Solomon *et al.* (eds.), *Sensory Deprivation: A Symposium* (Cambridge, Mass.: Harvard University Press, 1961), pp. 222, 225, 228, 229.
4. E. Berne, *Games People Play* (New York: Grove Press, Inc., 1967), p. 15.
5. Maurice L. Farber, *Theory of Suicide* (New York: Funk & Wagnalls, 1968), p. 47. Italics his.
6. *Ibid.,* p. 49.
7. *Ibid.,* p. 29.

Chapter 5   *Fear*

1. The reference is to the novel *Rebecca* by Daphne du Maurier.
2. William James, *Pragmatism* (London: Longmans, Green, 1908), pp. 12–13.

3. John Bowlby, *Child Care and the Growth of Love* (Harmondsworth: Penguin Books, 1955), p. 75.

Chapter 6   *The Meaning of Persons*

1. John Locke, *An Essay Concerning Human Understanding*, II, 27, 9.
2. Carl R. Rogers, *Client-Centered Therapy* (Boston: Houghton-Mifflin, 1951), p. 498. Italics his.
3. *Ibid.*, p. 500.
4. Henri Bergson, *The Two Sources of Morality and Religion* trans. R. Ashley Audra & C. Brereton (New York: Doubleday, 1935), p. 49.
5. This mutuality is a kind of sharing, a procedure which plays an important part in Tournier's therapeutic work. I have drawn attention to this in a short article entitled "On Speaking of Oneself," *Pastoral Psychology,* Vol. 21, No. 205 (June 1970), pp. 46–49.

Chapter 7   *Guilt*

1. See Lewis G. Sherrill, *Guilt and Redemption* (Richmond, Virginia: John Knox Press, 1963).
2. Karen Horney, *Our Inner Conflicts* in *The Collected Works of Karen Horney* (New York: Norton, 1964), Vol. 1, pp. 42–43. Italics hers.
3. Edward V. Stein, *Guilt: Theory and Therapy* (Philadelphia: The Westminster Press, 1968), p. 14. Italics his.

Chapter 8   *Malaise and Rebirth*

1. L. W. Grensted, *Psychology and God* (London: Longmans, Green and Co., 1931), p. 94.
2. R. S. Lee, *Psychology and Worship* (London: S. C. M. Press, 1953), pp. 58–59.

Chapter 10   *Comment and Response*

1. See Michael Balint, *The Doctor, His Patient and the Illness* (New York: International Universities Press, 1957).
2. *Ibid.,* p. 216.
3. Gregory Baum, "Truth in the Church—Küng, Rahner, and Beyond," *The Ecumenist,* Vol. 9, No. 3 (March–April 1971), p. 42.

4. Herbert Fingarette, *The Self in Transformation* (New York: Harper & Row, 1965), p. 276.
5. M. Balint, *op. cit.*, p. 299. Italics his.
6. Personal communication.
7. John Bennett, *Social Salvation* (New York: Scribners, 1935), p. 53.

Index